MIND
OVER WATER

———————————◆———————————

Lessons on Life from the
Art of Rowing

Craig Lambert

A Marc Jaffe Book

A MARINER BOOK
HOUGHTON MIFFLIN COMPANY
BOSTON · NEW YORK

First Mariner Books edition 1999

For information about permission to reproduce selections
from this book, write to Permissions,
Houghton Mifflin Company, 215 Park Avenue South,
New York, New York 10003.

Library of Congress Cataloging-in-Publication Data
Lambert, Craig.
Mind over water : lessons on life from the art of
rowing / Craig Lambert.
p.   cm.
"A Marc Jaffe book."
ISBN 0-395-85716-3
ISBN 978-0-618-00184-2 (pbk.)
1. Lambert, Craig. 2. Rowers — United States — Biography.
3. Rowing. 4. Self-actualization (Psychology). I. Title.
XGV790.92.L35A3   1998
796.1'23'092 — dc21 [B] 98-34450 CIP

Printed in the United States of America

Book design by Robert Overholtzer

DOH 10 9 8

for L.W.L. and R.K.L.,
and to she who has inspired me

✦

Contents

The Steersman

In the long run men hit only what they aim at.
Therefore, though they should fail immediately,
they had better aim at something high.

— THOREAU, *Walden*

IN THE DARKNESS, deep in silence, the lights — green, red, a few of white — surge ahead, in the rhythm of breathing. They seem, in fact, to breathe their way forward, gathering force on the inhale, then gliding forward on the outward stroke. Against the dark water and the shore, whatever propels these lights is indistinct, but their graceful flow suggests swans.

Now one swan swims closer, and if this be waterfowl, it is ancient, prehistoric, fantastically long and narrow, a pterodactyl afloat. Its beak juts out ten feet or more, and the wingspan sweeps a tremendous arc, fifteen or sixteen feet across. Two wings beat together, a *whoosh* through the river water. As they emerge into air and recoil for another immense stroke, it becomes clear: these are no wings. They are oars.

As waves of dread wash through my gut, I watch the colored lights from the ramp that leads from the boathouse down to the dock. Soon, red and green beacons of my own, attached to the bow of my boat, will float beside these others, just inches above the river surface. I am about to become the heart and muscle of one of

3

these sleek water birds. How, I wonder, did I get myself into this predicament?

It is 5:45 A.M. on an October morning in Boston, and both air and water are chilly. Already my hands ache with cold and I have yet to shove off from the dock; on the river, the frigid breeze will penetrate skin, flesh, and bone. That much is familiar: nothing more than intense, torturous pain. As a rower I am used to that. The terrifying thing is the athletic test confronting me: a double Head, something I have never attempted before and am not sure that I can even do, let alone do well. Performing well matters deeply, but today my first concern is staying alive out there. That, and the traffic.

The phrase *double Head* first caught my attention several years earlier, in a snatch of overheard conversation that crystallized the vast gap between my rowing practices and those of the top athletes in the sport. Two members of my boat club, Kurt Somerville and Tiff Wood, had been chatting after a row. Kurt, a downtown lawyer, is a tall, lanky oarsman who rowed at Dartmouth and then made the 1980 U.S. Olympic team, those unlucky athletes Jimmy Carter made into spectators. Kurt's nickname is "Wedge." He explains: "a wedge is the simplest tool."

Tiff Wood is another rowing tool; in college, his nickname was "the Hammer." Actually, many oarsmen have been called hammers, crew slang for rowers who lack finesse. Like *ringer,* the term *hammer* blends censure and praise: although hammers are crude implements, they can, of course, come in very handy. Tiff's untamed technique didn't stop him from becoming one of the great oarsmen of his era. After a spectacular career at Harvard, where his crews never lost a race, Tiff made the 1976, 1980, and 1984 U.S. Olympic teams and became one of the most famous names in rowing.

As the two Olympians talked, I listened in disbelief as Kurt uttered four innocent-sounding words: "Tiff: Saturday — double Head?"

This simple phrase stunned me. Kurt was casually proposing that, on Saturday, he and Tiff go out in their single sculls and row a double Head piece together. To my ears, he might as well have said, "Tiff: Saturday — climb Mount Everest?" On the Charles River, to row "a Head piece" means to row the full three-mile course of the Head of the Charles Regatta, a demanding endeavor that can take as little as fourteen minutes in an eight-oared boat or seventeen minutes in a single scull. It can also take well over twenty minutes. That doesn't sound so terribly long, but think of it as, say, running four or five consecutive four-minute miles.

Actually, it might be even tougher. Unlike running, rowing calls on every major muscle group in the body — legs, buttocks, back, abdomen, shoulders, arms — and pits them against resistance. Activating so much muscle tissue at once generates a tremendous demand for oxygen that sets your lungs on fire. Listening to Kurt and Tiff, I recalled my own scorched lungs while racing in the Head of the Charles, one of the most demanding things I had ever done. Now a *double* Head — a six-mile monster, two Head pieces back-to-back — was something I'd never heard of anyone doing. It seemed, in fact, an impossible feat. *Double Head?* I thought. *Sure you are.*

Hence my dread. As the boat lights glide by on this cool, dark Tuesday morning, I myself am about to attempt the impossible: a double Head. The Head of the Charles Regatta has accepted a few dozen of us from Cambridge Boat Club as competitors. The race is about three weeks away, and fifteen of us who are either taking it more seriously than the others, or desperately seizing all possible advantages, are out here preparing for the big test.

The Head of the Charles is the world's largest regatta; this year it will involve 16 events, 800 boats, 4,000 athletes, and perhaps more than 250,000 spectators. Rowers all over North America are preparing for this race, as are others in the British Isles, Europe, South America, Australia, and New Zealand. Many are no doubt rowing on their own bodies of water at this very moment. Here at Cambridge Boat Club we have been training for the Head for months and in the last few weeks have cranked up our intensity. Most of us are working out at least six days a week, just as we have all year long, but now we are really leaning into it.

I am in the best shape of my life, but for conditioning I am nowhere near the top of this Cambridge pack. Unfortunately, I'm not near the top on technique, size, strength, or experience, either. In a nutshell, I am dog-slow, one of the least competitive scullers of our training group.

Still, it is something to be rowing in the Head of the Charles at all. Of the millions of rowers in the world, only a small fraction have ever competed in this race, the pinnacle of the autumn rowing calendar. I am a masters rower, officially defined as anyone over age thirty. I have comfortably cleared that hurdle. As a forty-seven-year-old sculler, I am one of fifty entrants in the men's Senior Masters Single event, for oarsmen from forty through forty-nine. *Single* refers to the type of boat, a racing shell rowed by one person. Simply put, I am competing at the lowest end of the highest end of the sport.

In preparing for the Head, our Cambridge cohort is getting help from Gordon Hamilton, a rowing coach retained by the club to coach its advanced and competitive scullers. The Hamiltons are a true rowing family; Gordon's brother Chuck has coached crew at Mount Hermon School in western Massachusetts since 1970, and his eldest brother, Henry, is a well-known oarsman who runs his own sculling camp each summer. All three belong to Cambridge Boat Club.

Henry is a wiry, accomplished sculler who won the Senior Masters Single in 1988. In his time, Henry had been the rowing equivalent of a ski bum. At fifty-three, he remains an unrepentant river rat: since serving with the Navy in Vietnam, he has never done anything but row, coach, and work on boats. But while the popularity of skiing pumps money into many businesses, rowing is a tiny, elite sport that supports only a trickle of commerce. Consequently, for some time Henry lived out of his VW van — chilly in winter, but rent-free. One of its favorite mooring spots was the Cambridge Boat Club parking lot.

Gordon Hamilton has a wife, child, and full-time coaching job at M.I.T. Though not a complete oarhead, he is addicted to coaching, one of those enslaved persons who is compelled to advise athletes. For example, one morning when I was sculling downstream, Gordon passed me, heading upstream in a motor launch behind his group of scullers. Bound by the custom of mutual observation that governs all of us who promenade the Charles River, Gordon had reviewed my rowing form. Unable to help himself, he spun his launch around, followed me downstream a few hundred yards, and told me to get my hands away from the body quicker at the finish of the stroke. After tracking me long enough to see that his advice had registered, Gordon did another U-turn and rejoined his group.

For several weeks before the Head of the Charles, Gordon is taking our group out to train twice a week. On this Tuesday, once we have launched our singles, he explains how the double Head will work. We'll begin at the finish line of the racecourse and row a "reverse" Head piece downstream to the start, rowing at full pressure but at a slow cadence of 20–22 strokes per minute. Then we'll turn around and row the second Head piece upstream, again with full pressure but at a racing rate, which might be anywhere from 26 to 32 strokes per minute, depending on the athlete. Gordon will time the second piece with his stopwatch and give us our individual results at the finish line.

My time doesn't much concern me today, but survival does. To collapse and fail to finish the piece would mean humiliation in front of some of the best athletes in my sport. Not my idea of a good time. But my greatest anxiety is navigating the *traffic*.

Understand this: to stage a race for fifty boats, you cannot line everyone up at the starting line and yell, "Go!" For one thing, the Charles River is much too narrow for fifty racing lanes, and in any case the idea of setting up fifty buoyed lanes over a three-mile distance is ludicrous. To get eight hundred boats up the river on one fall day, you do something called a head race. The term comes from England, where college crews at Oxford and Cambridge compete each spring in "Head of the river" races that use a staggered start: the crew that has earned the right to lead the racing procession holds the honorific title of "head of the river." In America, a head race is one rowed against the clock, with a staggered start. In the Head of the Charles, the boats start at ten-second intervals and are timed by a computer over the course. The fastest time wins. That way, you need only one racing lane, albeit a wide one.

It has to be wide. The staggered start still puts quite a few boats on the river at once. Naturally, everyone would like to steer the shortest possible course to the finish line, and so, in theory, all boats would prefer that one optimal pathway through the water. The trouble starts when a faster shell overtakes a slower one on the course. The rules require the slower boat to give way. But sometimes the slower boat refuses to admit that it is being passed and so does *not* give way. This situation can lead to some rude exchanges between athletes in the two boats.

But even when the slower shell is willing to move over, the maneuvering can still be tricky. If someone is about to pass you, you need to (1) see them coming early enough to adjust your course, (2) determine their probable course and clear out of their way in a timely manner, (3) move far enough away to avoid clashing oars, an ugly event that can slow both boats, stop both boats, or even flip a boat over, while you (4) minimize your own divergence from the ideal course. To complicate matters, sometimes two or more boats may be closing on you at once. Steering through river traffic of this density at racing speed can present some unnerving problems. The worst-case scenario, a collision, is unlikely to prove fatal — except to one's chances in the race and to those of one's unhappy antagonist. Boat crashes can launch some floating conversations that are notably short on pleasantries.

We begin the double Head piece. One nice thing about tackling such an endeavor is that once begun, there is nothing to do but finish it. In rowing, launching commits you. There is no diving overboard and swimming back to shore, much as you may feel like it at times; no matter how hard the workout is, you *are* going to complete the task. The lack of any real alternative serves up the bracing tonic of decisiveness: one's course is clear, since there is no other.

Out on the river, my anxieties about what *might* happen give way to the stronger claims of what *is* happening. When rowing a shell, there is so much to pay attention to, and the consequences of *not* paying attention are so immediate and so drastic, that the task forces you into the present moment and holds you there. Reality trumps reverie. In this respect, crew resembles auto racing, another activity that requires total alertness. Racing through traffic produces intense physical and mental stress; thus, it is essential to relax the body as often as possible. Relaxing the mind is fatal.

My downstream piece at a slow cadence goes well enough. It tires my muscles a bit but also loosens me up. We turn the boats around and align ourselves for the upstream piece, the "real" one. Gordon starts us in reverse order of our estimated speed: the slowest scullers at the front of the pack. (I start second.) This is a reasonable scheme that keeps everyone roughly together on the river; if the fastest people went off first, they would simply row away from everybody else, and the slower boats would soon be rowing along in forlorn solitude.

Yet there is a fiendish consequence to this starting order. For our group of scullers, it means that by the time we reach the two-and-a-half-mile mark, the very fastest boats will be overtaking the very slowest boats: then and there, the contrast in speed will be maximal. But at this very spot, the river narrows and veers sharply left as it passes under the Eliot Bridge. The bridge has three arches, and the race course goes through the middle one. The confluence of a narrow stream, a sharp turn, and the squeeze through the center arch spells trouble. On race day, many crashes have occurred at this spot as two or even three crews tried to jockey through the center arch side by side and proved unable to stay clear of each other. The Cambridge Boat Club membership has enjoyed an excellent view of these thrilling mishaps since its boathouse looks out at this very point on the Charles.

My upstream Head piece gets off nicely. I come up to speed well before the starting line, so I can approach the start at close to racing pace. As I cross the line, in front of the Boston University boathouse, Gordon yells, "Row!" and I really hit it. Within a quarter mile I pass the one boat ahead of me and so briefly lead the pack, but over the next mile several boats go by me. This is no surprise; I expect these faster scullers to be speeding by, and I steer out of their way successfully. My goal is simply to row a good race and steer a good course. So far, I have handled the traffic well.

But then comes the treacherous Eliot Bridge. As I approach the center arch, three of the fastest scullers in the pack are bearing down on me. Kurt Somerville's boat is hurtling up the river on my starboard side. On my port side is Tom Darling, a former Olympian whose single is coming on like a bat out of hell. And heading directly for me, rowing hard, is the redoubtable Henry Hamilton, piloting a dark green torpedo aimed directly at my stern.

As I approach the bridge, there is nowhere to go — I am hemmed in from behind and on both sides. Steer to port, and I obstruct Tom; move to starboard, I am in Kurt's way; if I stay the course, Henry's shell will soon be in my lap. How to escape these guys — row faster? *I am already rowing as fast as I can.* The only option seems to be levitation: find a joystick in my boat, pull back, lift off, and fly a few feet above the water as the three shells speed past beneath me.

But there is no joystick; the only sticks that can make this boat fly are my oars. Pressure like this rivets your attention wonderfully, and one priority now shines with burning clarity: *get through the arch before they do.* Whatever problems I already have with this pursuit squadron will worsen drastically if they catch me under the bridge. The arch has room for, at most, two shells abreast. The idea of four boats trying to squeeze themselves through that opening is unthinkable.

It is time to go savage. I take my rate up for the next fifteen strokes and pour everything I have onto the oarblades. When I emerge from the Eliot Bridge, unscathed and still a few feet ahead of the posse, I feel like a prisoner who has wriggled through a narrow passageway to freedom. On the other side of the bridge the river widens, and from there on, all courses are about equal in their distance to the finish line. I veer my shell to starboard and see Kurt doing the same; he goes past me on that side as Tom and Henry zoom by on port. I am out of danger, and all that remains is to row hard for the last half mile.

Past the finish line the scullers are spent. The boats paddle lazily along as their human engines relax and breathe in a slower rhythm as they blow off any carbon dioxide residue from the race. *Muscle exhaust.* Soaked in sweat and a pleasant fatigue, some just stop and drink from their water bottles. It's a time to review what happened over the course. I have been through a battle, and it was harrowing. Under pressure I had been frantic but didn't crack; I kept my wits and made choices that worked, both for me and the nearby boats. I had competed among the great athletes. Not *against* them, really, but *among* them. I had steered through traffic. Today, that is surely enough.

Gordon drives his launch over to the boats and gives each of us our time; mine is actually the fastest Head piece I have rowed. It sinks in: I have done a double Head, the feat that once seemed superhuman. Not only that, but my performance was a personal best. Fighting through race traffic probably increased my speed.

Then the moment under the bridge flashes back, the instant when I thought, *I am already rowing as fast as I can.* Just seconds later, *I had rowed faster.*

We are out here in the darkness to reveal ourselves, to discover who we are. With the oars, we attempt things that we cannot do, we confront that which is beyond our capacities. *Mind over water.* The shells transport us into the unknown.

Edges form outlines. If our boundaries determine our identities, then we learn who we are by finding our limits. Rowing is a vehicle for finding them: it takes us into that nebulous zone where what I *can* do shades into that which I *cannot* do, where our abilities confront our aspirations. Which are more real?

Like any worthwhile adventure, this quest can be daunting. Reaching the end of our capacities inevitably means pain and reminds us that despite yearnings, we are not yet infinite. Any confrontation with one's limits reminds us of another, less negotiable limit. Yet our only alternative is standstill. Growth is uncomfortable; it results only from that which challenges us. Why does expanding our capacities matter so much? Perhaps we are rowing toward something other than the horizon, an unknown shoreline. Each stroke pulls us farther along an inner journey. The real voyage, whatever the boat, is into the soul.

For those of us who power these slender shells, a paramount goal is the full exploration of our talents. Otherwise only the demented would be afloat on the Charles River in the dim light before dawn. Something pulls us out of a warm bed into the cold darkness: call it a will to excel, or at least to accelerate, which on the water may come to the same thing. Speed afloat is a worthy motive. Still, it doesn't seem to rule out the "demented" explanation. What is so important about speed?

Our love for speed is not just a cultural trait, even if postmodern society is an urban racetrack where attention spans are short and everyone seems to be hurrying toward nowhere in particular. The ancient Greeks also loved speed and awarded laurel wreaths to the fastest runners in their Olympic Games.

Speed appeals to humanity for several reasons. First, being able to get somewhere faster than someone else confers a Darwinian advantage in competing for resources; speed helps one outrun predators, whether prehistoric beasts or downtown muggers, and to commandeer food and other useful goods. In case of violence or warfare, speed helps, both in avoiding conflicts and winning them.

Speed feels good. It is exhilarating to move fast. There is the sensual pleasure of the wind on the skin and the sound of water rushing beneath the hull, the pleasing bodily sensation of momentum. Speed also excites us because it is dangerous. The higher the speed, the less time to react in event of a mishap — and so the greater the danger and thrill. Rowing fast, one's bow driving up out of the water, feels like hydroplaning, even flying, and so woos us with the dream of flight. Freedom from gravity, from physical laws, beckons from the prow of speed, with the promise of ascent into higher realms.

Speed is also beautiful. To go fast demands efficiency, and efficiency jettisons all but the essential. Speed streamlines, sculpts a simplicity of line, designs elegance. True, many runners and rowers do go fast without any particular grace. They are exceptions, but we must credit them with discovering their own route into swiftness; on the medal stand, speed is a science, not an art. There is no single way to go fast any more than there is one formula for beauty. What ultimately matters is using your own talents fully, developing your own body and mind in a way that extracts their optimal velocity.

Rowing is a vehicle for exploring the outer limits of human performance. It occurs within a simplified context that permits a clear view of what is effective and what is not. In crew there is no defense, only offense: winning boat races simply means moving faster than everybody else. You cannot slow down your opponents. Since your sole weapon is speed, the goal is straightforward: maximize forward velocity. As it turns out, lessons learned afloat carry over onto dry land, where we also want maximal forward motion in our lives.

This does not mean charging pell-mell through life, chasing ill-considered goals, never pausing to enjoy the moment. Quite the opposite. Life at "full speed ahead" means realizing your ambitions in the shortest possible time. To do this requires us to know clearly what we want and to inhabit the present moment fully. We need to establish specific rituals that force us to become more fully alive. We learn to remove impediments, to gather momentum, to minimize friction. Reach your goals faster and you can realize more of your dreams in a lifetime — and so more rapidly fulfill your personal destiny. Life at high velocity speeds your own evolution.

Reaching the highest levels of performance usually requires us to compete with others. How can we improve our chances of winning? We race as single scullers as well as in crews of two, four, or eight rowers. Victories by rowing crews, like other crews, generally result from teamwork. A fast boat of eight rowers and a cox attains a power that transcends its nine separate individuals. Maximizing speed via concerted effort, we create outcomes where everyone profits. Such results build strong relationships with partners, teammates, and coaches — or, in different settings, with customers, voters, or investors.

At other times we operate in the zero-sum mode and seek to vanquish our opponents: *we* win, *they* lose: we *beat* them. Although it may seem old-fashioned, in regattas, proxy fights, and Olympic finals, this is still the preferred result, and in war it has no rival. A boat race is a civilized form of war. The big win grows from a series of smaller ones. Conquering the other crews — the external opponents — means at every moment winning smaller battles within yourself.

In the boats, we explore the concepts that underlie creation. Like Einstein, we wish to know God's thoughts. We shall attempt to pry them loose with an oar. The raw elements of the sport are our teachers: the wind and the water, the boat and its oars, our own bodies and minds.

In the shell we occupy a liminal area between sky and water, between carp and cormorant. The rower is both fish and bird — a flying fish, or else an aquatic condor with a staggering wingspan, skimming across the water's surface. Suspended between liquid and air, we inhabit a transitional zone that opens a window on mysteries hidden from those with solid ground beneath their feet. Sliding between dark and shadow, between sunlight and the obscure, is the region of discovery. Here the inchoate seeks form. Every area of creation has such a penumbra: venture capital, avant-garde arts, courtship. In such crucibles, imagination creates the future.

The penumbral zone offers *optimal unpredictability*. Consider avant-garde music. The radical compositions of John Cage, using randomness, ambient sound, and noise, are too unpredictable for most audiences. The listener cannot relate the sounds to any known pattern (since they are patternless by design) and so has trouble making sense of the music. The result is boredom and disinterest. At the other extreme, a children's song like "Twinkle, Twinkle, Little Star" is too predictable. Listeners know the melody by heart, again producing disengagement.

Partial unpredictability, *semi*-understandability, engage our attention. This is the region of learning. Take blues music, which uses a twelve-bar pattern of chord changes known as the "blues twelve." Within that pattern a musician can improvise, creating new melodic lines, rhythms, and harmonies. For many audiences, blues improvisation strikes that optimal balance between the known and unknown; it is just unpredictable enough. But beauty is in the ear of the listener. A sophisticated audience may find a standard blues too predictable and require more progressive music that strains against familiar forms.

Rowing, too, has its traditional forms: we row within a community and a history. It would be foolish for me to act as if I were the first person ever to try to perfect my sculling, to wrestle with the challenges posed by a tippy boat and rough water. Others have worked over these problems long before I was born. We have mentors. Through the decades, rowing champions and great coaches have discovered and refined certain principles that produce extraordinary levels of performance. They have learned how to create the results they envisioned, turning an idea into a physical reality. This is a near-godlike faculty, and in fact, rowers do refer to such outstanding performers as *gods.* Luckily, since these deities still walk the earth, they can offer us divine guidance.

Rowing is such a beautifully small, obscure sport; in the rowing community, as in a village, everyone knows everyone else. Consequently, a journeyman like myself can train alongside the best players alive — past and present Olympians, genuine world-class athletes. Very few sports are like this. Imagine being a playground basketball player who, every day, gets to shoot hoops with Michael Jordan; or a club tennis player warming up each morning next to Pete Sampras and Steffi Graf, getting tips from Steffi on your slice backhand. At Cambridge Boat Club, that is what I do five or six mornings a week, seven or eight months a year. My rowing friends, coaches, and acquaintances have been to the Henley Royal Regatta, the World Championships, the Olympic Games. Some are heading toward the next Olympics. They have won gold, silver, and bronze medals at all levels of the sport and on lakes and rivers all over the world.

My own medal collection is limited. It's limited to fantasies since I haven't won any. True, as an oarsman on an eight-oared crew, I have won some races. And I was once Cambridge Boat Club's novice sculling champion. That blistering competition had only one other entrant; it was a race in which you finished either first or last. I finished first. Regrettably, there was no medal ceremony, so I had to content myself with the ensuing fame and glory. Most of that had dissipated by the time I reached the dock.

But if I have not been a champion, I have surely lived among them, and there has been much to learn in their midst. The greatest rowers have pushed not only their personal limits but the limits of *human* capacities. They have probed the high end of performance, have taken the human vehicle to a kind of zenith. Their rituals can show us a path to doing likewise.

Tonight I steer the boat upstream into the twilight, on this November evening in 1965. Along its serpentine course, the Charles River widens and narrows, and its riparian sounds swell to crescendos in places or relax to the low purr of a river at peace. Downstream, where the current winds through Boston, hard skyscraper surfaces blast the roar of the city's traffic out onto the river. Travel upstream through the academic burg of Cambridge and the din abates as the river narrows, like the roads along its banks. Farther west, another diminuendo ensues in suburban Watertown, where herons wade the shallows. Tonight it is quiet indeed. This particular evening will soon get even quieter, perhaps quieter tonight than it will be for the rest of the twentieth century.

We have rowed well into Watertown, having launched downstream from Newell Boathouse, home of the Harvard men's crew. We are newcomers to Newell, trying out for the freshman crew. There are nine of us in this boat, and most of us don't know what we are doing. We are all male, all freshmen, all seventeen or eighteen years old. Beyond that we have little in common. We come from all parts of the United States. Most of us attended public high schools and had never been in a racing shell until we arrived at Harvard a few weeks ago.

Four of the eight oarsmen, however, do have rowing experience, some of them several years of it. These are young men from wealthier families, the preppies, boys from private schools that had boats, boathouses, and crews. Far more accomplished rowers than the rest of us, they radiate the exasperation of privileged teenagers thrown together with five other boys who, like me, are rank beginners at their sport. Unfortunately, our incompetence affects them directly.

The German word for *coxswain* is *Steuermann,* steersman. As coxswain it is my task to steer this mixed pack of purebreds and mongrels. In the twilight I sit in the sternmost seat, controlling not an oar but a rudder, a wooden flap attached to our stern. I must navigate our course and avoid obstacles like bridge abutments and other shells. In each hand I grip a wooden handle on a rope that controls the rudder.

I also must keep the boat from tipping to port or starboard, and

I am just learning that this is crucial in rowing. The balance or level of the boat is called its *set*, and when the boat is *set up*, it is, metaphorically, on an even keel. It is not literally on one because racing shells do not have keels; a keel would slow the boat down intolerably. But here, as elsewhere, speed exacts its price: with no keel for stability, the shell lists easily.

So rowing this boat demands a delicate balance. Just as when walking a tightrope, you must keep your body precisely centered; throw your weight even slightly to one side or another and severe trouble immediately ensues. Crew makes two seemingly incompatible demands. You are doing gruntwork, heavy muscular effort, pulling on the oars — yet, you must maintain a tenuous balance that requires continuous fine adjustments in your physical position. So not only is it like walking a tightrope but like lifting a barbell at the same time.

The inexperienced boys on this freshman crew don't know much about setting up a shell. This evening our boat often lists to port, which makes rowing an ordeal, especially for the port side oarsmen. The careening shell jams their oars far too deep into the river and makes them struggle to get them out. One port oar is the crew's stroke, a handsome, tall, blond preppie who faces me directly. From three feet away he snarls, "*We're down to port!*" with the plain implication that I should do something about it. *Like what?* Through my small megaphone, I tell the crew that we are down to port, but nothing changes. Then it does change: they overcorrect and we are down to starboard. Next, the boat sets up for a couple of strokes, but then we go down to port again. This Sisyphean cycle only amplifies the stroke's frustration.

While the unbalanced shell is the key irritant, I can also feel the stroke's displeasure at having a cox who doesn't immediately recognize the problem and take steps to correct it. For him, tonight's row feels like thrashing around in a washtub full of bozos, a major step backward from the smooth crew he rowed with last year at St. Paul's. I'm letting him down: *I'm no coxswain, I don't know how to get these guys to set up a shell.* For now, however, we are all in this boat together.

How did I get myself into this mess? Like so many messes, it started with following rules. Harvard imposed a physical education requirement on freshmen: thirty times per semester we were required to show up for an athletic activity of our choice. We could sample from a wide selection of sports and activities, but a simple way to accumulate jock credits was to go out for a freshman team, since there was practice five days a week. That incentive drew me to Newell Boathouse.

There were also deeper reasons. In my four years of high school in New Jersey, I had never played a varsity sport. I had been a very active student, involved in a wide variety of activities both in and out of school, and, like many Harvard freshmen, I had the best academic record in my high school class. At seventeen, my confidence in my mental abilities was strong. But I profoundly disbelieved in myself as an athlete. In high school I was convinced that I was not good enough to make a team: I couldn't play with the big boys, couldn't hope to measure up to *real* athletes. In our youth, many of us form surprisingly strong, durable beliefs about our limits — convictions regarding what we are not, and what we cannot do.

In the New Jersey countryside of the 1950s and '60s, we boys played sports, all kinds of sports: baseball, football, basketball, soccer, swimming, bowling, tennis, even golf. Most of our play was of the sandlot variety, since adults had not yet taken over children's sports. In those innocent days, only kids were on the field.

I lived in an area with open fields and vacant lots. We had no idea who owned them, but we knew we were welcome to play there. Such open spaces were a community resource of sorts, even if they were privately owned; lawyers had not yet advised the landholders that they might be liable for a million-dollar lawsuit if one of the boys were to twist his ankle in a rabbit hole that had been negligently left unfilled. The outdoors was not childproofed, yet kids were welcome to play.

We lived in a residential area surrounded by a large forest. The woods made our neighborhood an enclave, a village of about thirty families. The young boys of this little community played together every day. In the fall, we might start up a game of touch football on the rolling expanse of someone's backyard. We improvised sidelines and endlines — trees, shrubs, and big rocks figuring heavily in the dimensions — and invented rules, using the official version of each sport as a kind of template. On questionable calls we negotiated. Since there were no adult umpires to adjudicate, we learned to compromise and get along or play would not continue. And sometimes it didn't: a boy might "pick up his marbles and go home," declaring that if others would not play by his rules, he was leaving the community. The individual ego and the group's will could clash even over a game of hide-and-seek.

But mostly the play went on. I played in all these games and also spent hours alone, absorbed in things like throwing a hollow pink rubber ball against the side of our garage — pitching at targets, fielding the rebounds, playing out full nine-inning baseball games in my imagination. I threw either right-handed or left-handed, depending on which major league pitcher I wanted to emulate that day. It was always a pitcher from that greatest of all teams, the Brooklyn Dodgers, the club my father had taught me to love.

I also spent days near our crabapple tree, hitting fruit. The tree was enormous, and each year it dropped thousands of crabapples onto the ground, spheres the size and color of cherries but hard as apples. I had a small brown wooden bat that my parents had given me, and on a summer day I could spend a rapt hour or two tossing crabapples into the air and hitting them for distance and average. The reddish stain on the fat part of the bat showed I was connecting in the right location. Since crabapples were only one-tenth the size of baseballs, this arboreal batting practice taught me an accurate swing.

I played only one "organized" sport, baseball, in a summer recreational league sponsored by the country township we lived in. I was a catcher, a position I had liked ever since seeing a Cleveland Indians catcher in a game at Yankee Stadium. The catcher's equipment seemed like a knight's armor, and it was a position with a lot of action, since you were involved in every pitch.

Best of all, a catcher gets to complete the most exciting play in baseball: a play at the plate, the moment of life or death — either a run scores or the runner is *Out!* In one twilight game I tagged out two boys trying to score; reviewing the game afterward, a teammate's father noted that the second play had been close but the first kid was "out like a light." I had enjoyed flipping the switch.

As a young athlete, I was what I remain today: a good all-arounder. While I have never been great at any sport, I have generally been good at most of them. In baseball I threw accurately, if not for distance; I caught balls well and was reliable on defense. As a hitter I rarely struck out, carrying a good batting average since I could make contact and hit line drives into the outfield. But I was no power hitter; a two-base hit was a big deal, and home runs were rare. My foot speed was only average because, although my leg muscles were strong, the legs themselves were short. In football I had sure hands for catching passes — when I could get clear of the defender — and I could throw short passes accurately. I rarely ran the ball, and as one of the smallest boys, I was of little use on the line. In playground basketball I seldom won a rebound and, on defense, found that taller boys easily shot over me; yet I dribbled and passed well, could find open men, and had a respectable outside shot. Furthermore, unlike some of my frustrating teammates, I rarely blew lay-ups. Even with this mixed array of skills I was a better-than-average athlete, since most boys had similarly uneven talents but practiced less than I did.

However, in the hierarchical world of young boys, certain athletic skills outrank others. The slugger who belts a home run is more impressive than the singles hitter who reaches base and therefore scores on the homer, no matter that both runs count equally on the scoreboard. A quarterback who throws bullet passes attracts more notice than the tight end who returns to the huddle to explain that the defense is leaving the short secondary open, so a pass there will succeed. The tall boy who can dunk the basketball will be chosen long before the short point guard who hits an open forward with a backdoor pass, even if both plays score two points. As we grew up, we learned how team sports really worked and began to notice who had useful talents in certain roles. But during my early youth, it was I who was the singles hitter, the tight end, the point guard, a boy with valuable but unspectacular skills.

Simply put, little boys resemble American sports spectators, and vice versa. Few actually grasp the underlying dynamics of the game, but everyone absorbs the spectacle. And in the television era the spectacle sells, both to the viewing audience on their couches and to boys in sandlots.

There is spectacle, and there is size. To males, size matters, and the younger they are — whatever their chronological age — the more it matters. This fact held sway when we chose up sides for a game, especially if the players included new boys who had not seen me play. The two team captains tossed a coin or stacked hands up a bat for first pick, and from then on they alternately chose boys in an order strongly correlated with stature. In the recreational baseball league or at school, where teachers formed the teams, I was selected to play just like everyone else. But in sandlot games I dreaded this ritual; as the shortest boy or nearly so, I inevitably was one of the last chosen.

Why does this choosing-up rite matter so? The primitive draft begins with everyone standing together in a group, all of us on an equal footing. Then, like the nucleus of an amoeba dividing in two, the team captains somehow emerge and assert themselves. The leaders walk a few paces away from the group, begin the selection ritual, and the mitosis continues; the entire social organism splits into two camps. As he is chosen, each boy goes to stand behind his leader, and eventually with his team as the choices accumulate.

The sequence of selection establishes an athletic class system, a pecking order. The draft clearly and publicly ranks desirability; we who were repeatedly passed over soon learned where we stood. As the teams filled out, I would sag in misery as the common pool dwindled and neither side had claimed me. The dismay recalled that of the children's game Musical Chairs, which teaches scarcity: *you may be the one left out.* To be the last boy chosen, as I sometimes was, stigmatized me as the least desired athletic asset in the community. *I can't play with the big boys.*

If I was often at the bottom of this totem pole, I was simultaneously learning to climb another pole, where I came out on top. From my earliest years I was a straight-A student; by fourth grade it was clear that, academically, I could at least equal the best of my peers and perhaps surpass them. School was a larger competitive arena that held both boys and girls, and we dimly recognized, even as children of seven or eight, that this playing field was the one that counted in the "real" world.

Teachers, too, ran contests, academic competitions such as spelling bees, which I frequently won. Perhaps the children who were less adroit with words felt a humiliation like mine in being passed over for a team when they misspelled a word and had to sit down. In a spelling bee, to be the last one left standing was victory, not rejection; you stood alone as king of the hill. From such experiences, as well as report cards and the thousand other comparisons and tests — raisings of hands, smiles from the teacher, displays of work — that take place in classrooms every day, I learned which side of my bread was buttered. If I wanted to be a winner — and what boy does not? — here was an arena where I could shine.

Friends recognized my academic talent and would ask me how to solve an arithmetic problem or enlist me to help them with homework. Through nine years of primary school, all at the same school with essentially the same classmates, I developed a reputation as a "brain." Hearing myself so described both pleased and annoyed me. It was flattering that someone recognized, even admired, my intelligence. But the compliment included a strain of disrespect, implying that if you were a "brain," you were limited to the cerebral side of life and, in fact, that was *all* you were good for. To identify someone with any single body part — be it mouth, legs, breasts, or brain — dismisses their value as a whole person. Having been stereotyped in this way, at once idealized and belittled, offered an early taste of what it might be like to be female or a member of a racial minority.

The left-handed compliment *he's a brain* reflects our opposition of mind and body, thought and action, intellect and sports. Our culture enshrines many tiresome stereotypes; among them is the "dumb jock," who excels on the playing field but is a dolt in the classroom or anywhere else that requires mental power. The jock's musculature supposedly continues above the neck. The inverse of the dumb jock is the nerd: the studious intellectual, who shines on exams, standardized tests, and transcripts but who is a thin, weak, clumsy incompetent, a fish out of water in sports. We have scant lore of smart jocks or vigorous nerds.

Such cultural icons do not exist in the abstract. They are real insofar as they dwell in our minds and souls, and these polarized types did indeed live in my psyche. They stood as guides to who I was and what I could become; if I was a smart boy, an "A student," a brain, someone who played chess and bridge well before age ten, then I was no athlete, no matter what the rest of me might say or do. Through the ancient techniques of carrot and stick, my friends and teachers pointed me toward scholarship, away from sports. I learned where investments of energy paid off in winning, success, and approval. While my friends and I continued to play sandlot games all through high school, these tapered off as other activities expanded. And the idea of organized sports, going out for my school's varsity teams, was something I never considered. True athletic competition was for a different class of people, the big boys, the real athletes. That, I knew, did not mean me.

Then I arrived at Harvard, where I encountered a menu of sports that no public high school could offer. There were sports — like squash, lacrosse, and crew — that I had never even seen, let alone tried. This was a new playing field, one where perhaps I could succeed.

In crew, I had heard about one position where small size was actually an asset: the coxswain. Eight rowers pulled oars and in that sense literally "pulled their weight," but the ninth crew member, the coxswain, had no oar. He steered the boat, gave orders to the crew, and coordinated the group effort. Some called the cox the "brain" of the crew — would this epithet dog me? — but coxswains were legitimate athletes who won varsity letters. Since the cox did *not* pull his weight, that weight should be minimal. Thus, coaches needed small boys as coxswains, and at seventeen I weighed only about 125 pounds. I later learned that this was actually a bit heavy for a cox, but in the fall of 1965, no one was asking us to weigh in. It was enough to show up at practice and be willing to steer eight thrashing oarsmen in a tippy boat through a freezing headwind.

The freshman coach had also been a coxswain. He was an intense character named Ted Washburn who had been the varsity cox at Harvard and whose crew went undefeated his senior year. The summer after graduating, he went to the Olympics, steering the United States' coxed four that finished seventh at the 1964 Games in Tokyo. That fall, Ted became Harvard's freshman heavyweight rowing coach and immediately produced an undefeated crew in the spring of 1965. We were his second group of hopefuls.

As a coach, Washburn went beyond the reasonable. For example, an incoming freshman whose vital statistics looked promising for crew — say, 6 feet 3 inches tall, 190 pounds — might find Ted waiting for him in front of the door to his room when, lugging a suitcase, he first arrived at Harvard. Washburn would be the first person the freshman met, beating out even the roommates.

Ted liked to be first, particularly at the finish line, and his crews also performed unreasonably well. Ted was a genius. At only twenty-three years of age he radiated confidence and authority, some perhaps gained during years of bossing around much bigger men, some attributable to inheritance: his father, Brad Washburn, was the famous mountaineer and photographer who was the director of Boston's Museum of Science for forty years.

One of Ted's favorite moments came at the very start of the fall semester, when he called a little meeting for freshmen interested in rowing and made his recruiting speech. Ted would stand before this group of boys, who were brimming with uncertainty, anxiety, and excitement, and tell them they needed a focus. Without a focus, the distractions of Harvard and Boston would prove overwhelming; you might go through college and age by four years without moving any closer to learning who you were, the real learning of the college experience. Here Ted was touching a nerve in the adolescent psyche; at this point in our lives, finding out "who we were" was surely the heart of the matter.

At this juncture Ted liked to tell a story made famous by Professor John Finley, a well-known classicist and beloved grandpaternal figure at Harvard. It seems there was a family who moved from Pennsylvania to northern California but, fearing their dog might not be able to adjust to the new climate and environment, gave him to friends before leaving. Several weeks later the dog showed up on their front porch in Sebastopol, California. Finley told his students: that dog is your soul. You can avoid it, move away from it, distract yourself, lose yourself in the most remote parts of the world. You can forget your soul but *it cannot forget you.* It will remember you wherever you go, and someday you will find it, panting, on your front porch.

Coxing is like surgery. To be a surgeon you must love to cut. Holding a razor-sharp scalpel in your hand, ready to slice open the living human body, you must be resolute. You cannot vacillate or wiggle or vary the depth of your incision as doubts or second thoughts redirect your hand. Instead, you must cut straight, sure, and clean — almost, in fact, eagerly. An indecisive cox, like an ambivalent surgeon, is worse than useless. Wherever he goes, with whatever he says or touches, he sows confusion and disorder. The coxswain must seize control, take command of the boat and crew long before the shell ever leaves the dock.

In the boathouse, the shells rest on racks four or five tiers high, the lowest ones stored at calf height and the highest above the shoulders of even the taller oarsmen. The cox directs the eight rowers in lifting a shell off the rack and carrying it down the ramp, across the dock, and setting it into the water. A mishap in this seemingly simple portage can damage a $25,000 boat and also undermine the crew's trust in its coxswain, a breach that can be more difficult to repair than any harm done to the shell.

Thus the coxswain's orders need to have a military clarity and simplicity. "Hands on!" commands the eight rowers, arrayed along the length of the shell, to take the appropriate handholds. "Lift!" and the shell rises off the rack. "To the shoulders!" and the crew lowers the boat to their shoulders, followed by "Walk it out!" which signals them to carry their shell out onto the dock.

Decisiveness is even more important on the water, where many more unruly factors come into play. The greater the degree of surrounding chaos, the more crucial it becomes to have confident leadership. This, no doubt, explains the rise of dictatorships, but a coxswain's tyranny is at least a benevolent one. By handling decisions like setting the course, the cox frees the rowers' energies for more immediate tasks. But for this to work, the crew must have faith in the steersman, must believe in the course they are on.

To steer a boat you must choose a course and commit to it. An eight-oared shell is about sixty feet long and responds sluggishly to the rudder. These boats do not turn on a dime, nor on a half dollar or even a manhole cover. Consequently the cox must anticipate, looking far ahead to a chosen destination, and begin the turns early. Steering involves finding a point, usually some landmark onshore, with which to align the bow. The sooner the steersman can choose that point — and the more distant that point can be — the better. An early commitment to a destination permits the most effective choice of heading and the most latitude for adjustments. Barring some drastic change in conditions, last-minute changes in course betray incompetence at the rudder.

Seamless, accomplished performance in complex artistic or sports activities involves a paradox: we must perceive the future while performing in the present. For example, playing a Beethoven piano sonata, I read the upcoming bars of music while playing the current notes with my hands; the density of incoming information is too great for me to notice what my fingers are doing. I leave that to the fingers themselves, and to the emotions.

Similarly, an ice hockey star like Wayne Gretzky sees what is *about* to happen as well as what *is* happening. Taking a wider view of events on the ice than most players, Gretzky notices that a teammate will soon be clear to rifle a pass to a certain point near the blue line — so Gretzky skates *now* to where the pass will be *then*. Seeing this, his teammate does make the pass, and Gretzky, having created the future he envisioned, takes the puck in the open and scores.

In the boats, steering an optimal course means perceiving the future and responding now to its demands; late reactions mean sharp, sudden turns at the expense of speed. Certain turns, like the leftward veer at the Eliot Bridge, are so sharp that the coxswain must move the rudder before the turn comes into view: the steersman must simply know the river and do it right. Cumulative experience enables the cox, in a sense, to steer blind.

The best course minimizes turning. Whether in a car, in a boat, or on a horse, turns slow us down; on the straightaways, we attain top speed. On the river, well-steered turns leave long, sweeping wakes behind them on the water. The simplest and straightest course is fastest, first because it travels the shortest distance between two points, second because it maximizes the benefit from the rowers' energies, applying their power to forward rather than sideways momentum.

You can also turn an eight without the rudder: the cox can command the rowers on either the port or starboard side of the boat to pull harder ("Hard on starboard!"), and this will turn the shell much more dramatically than a rudder can. But unbalanced pulling slows the boat markedly, for the same reasons noted above, and because the oars on one side must ease up. Even, steady pressure is the richest fuel.

A crew that trusts its coxswain will do as the cox asks automatically, without questioning the wisdom of the command. On the water, this type of autarchy is not only efficient but at times absolutely necessary. While training or during a race, the crew must sometimes take rapid action to avoid disaster, and again, as in surgery, there is no time for second thoughts or democratic debates. When the coxswain intones, "Weigh enough!" (the conventional command for *stop rowing*, derived from the nautical phrase under *weigh*, i.e., under *way*), the crew must obey instantly, perhaps to avoid hitting a floating log or a wayward boat coming from the other direction. (The coxswain's tone of voice conveys the degree of urgency.)

The crew's trust in their cox builds from a series of small accomplishments. *We lifted the boat off the rack, got it down the dock and into the water without anything weird happening.* There is a cumulative lesson learned: *do what the cox says and things work out well.* A cox who builds trust and belief in routine decisions can command obedience to bolder requests. Toward the end of a close race, rowing neck-and-neck against another boat with two hundred meters to go, the crew may feel that they are exerting themselves to the maximum. But then their coxswain commands, "Up two — in *two* — and we have them," and two strokes later, the rate rises from 38 to 40 per minute, and the race is won. The cox, the brain of the crew, pushed its eight bodies to do more than they realized they could do, just as our brains can with our individual bodies.

Simple as it sounds, a congruence of word and deed — doing what we say — is one starting place for building divine powers. *In the beginning was the word.* When I keep my word, my language incarnates itself. Realization, a *making real.* Eventually my word becomes law. He who does not keep his word is powerless: he says one thing and does another. Reality does not obey his commands. But for those who aspire to create their visions, deed and word agree; today's declaration becomes tomorrow's event. *And God said, Let there be light, and there was light.*

The order of events matters, for it gives primacy to language or physical reality, to consciousness or matter. If the deed comes first, we have *description;* when the word comes first, *creation.* This sequence distinguishes science from art, observation from innovation, sight from vision. Do we describe what we see, or do we create what we describe?

In creating reality, we train ourselves with small wins, which pave the way for bigger ones. The basic principle — *do what you say* — applies, regardless of the magnitude of the task.

Ted Washburn eventually became the preeminent freshman rowing coach in the United States. He has a gift for drama and is a superb storyteller who can make a fairly ordinary boat race seem like a titanic confrontation of good and evil, a *Götterdämmerung.* Stagecraft can sometimes set crews up for a big race.

Ted's position as mentor and leader made the crew more likely to credit his declarations, and Ted has a gift for reaching into the emotions of young men. At times he would play mind games with his crews. The day before a 2,000-meter race with Brown, for example, he might terrify his Harvard freshmen by warning them about how fast Brown was: "If you don't get at least a two-length lead on them by the 1,000-meter mark, they will take you in the second half." Scared of Brown's lurking speed, the Harvard freshmen would row especially hard, opening a big lead in the first half of the race — and then, over the last 1,000, continue to row away from Brown, which actually proved unable to mount any challenge. Harvard might do a "horizon job," winning by six boat lengths. (Rowers call such one-sided victories *horizon jobs,* a hyperbole suggesting that the margin of victory is so great that when the losing boat finishes, the winners have disappeared over the horizon.)

Thus Washburn had tricked his crew into performing at a level well beyond what they would have done had they known the "truth." Yet, what is the "truth" here? As athletes we also fool ourselves into *under*performing, through equally groundless beliefs concerning ourselves or our competitors.

Suppose Washburn's words and body language had instead convinced the crew, not that Brown was fast, but that they were very slow and that beating them would be a piece of cake. Complacent, Harvard might have stumbled into another scenario: Brown starts strongly and seizes the lead. Harvard, its expectations already demolished, fumbles, trying to regroup. Anxiety, even panic, seeps into their muscles, tension seizes up their oarblades. Meanwhile, Brown surges with confidence and a sense that the race is indeed winnable. In this scenario the outcome could be markedly different. Beliefs can rule outcomes, so wise coaches carefully choose what they tell their athletes. Wise athletes are equally selective about what they tell themselves.

Typically, the two converge: the coach's words echo in the athlete's mind. It looks as if the coach is in charge, acting as *cause* to the rower's *effect.* But remember that the athlete chooses to submit to the coach's power and to follow the coach's edicts. In this sense, the athlete is the point of origin, the one in charge.

Hence the question of *agency* arises: who is the active agent, the originating source? Clearly, athletes retain coaches for many reasons. For one thing, coaches personify an *external agency* that will drive the athletes to do more than they would on their own. In weight training, for example, assume an athlete is targeting ten to twelve repetitions of a bench press. But by the eighth rep the bar gets heavy, and the ninth rep requires special effort. Training alone, one might decide to stop there and put the bar onto its rests. But a coach stands nearby, saying "OK, that's nine, now *ten* — you can do it," and indeed the athlete squeezes out another lift. Then the coach says, "Just one more." Eventually the set goes to eleven or twelve reps instead of nine. Those last three stressful reps are the ones that really count, the ones that grow muscles. This is what the athlete wanted to do, but needed the coach, an external agent, to accomplish it. Who was responsible for those last few lifts? It is an elusive matter to resolve this question of agency, to find the ultimate steersman.

After winning an eight-oared race, the eight rowers and their coxswain are commonly hailed as the victors. Sometimes observers single out certain key performers — the stroke or cox, for example, and attribute the win to their efforts. Or the coach may get the credit. But every medal is an alloy, with many contributors: the designers and builders of the shell and oars; the boatman who rigged the shell, the assistant coach who transported all this equipment to the race site; friends and family who gave emotional sustenance; the cooks who fed the rowers; the farmers, sunlight, and water that grew the food that became their muscles. Each source is a tributary feeding the winning moment, adding an element necessary to the result. Viewing this conflux, one may contemplate the source behind these sources. The boat moves through both water and time. We can trace the river to its headwaters, but at the source of time, we float on a stream without banks, guided by another steersman.

Well upstream, in Watertown, we turn our boat around in the late twilight. The four oarsmen on the port side back their blades — rowing in reverse by pushing the oars away from them rather than pulling in — while their counterparts on starboard row normally, and the boat rotates. We row downstream, heading home in the darkness. The stroke's discomfiture has abated, mostly from resignation and partly because the rowers are slowly learning, through trial and error, how to set up the shell.

Ideally, the cox voices perceptions but not judgments. By giving feedback about how the boat feels in a tone that is engaged but neutral, the coxswain hands the rowers a problem and lets them find a solution. The crew will learn at its fastest rate if it can perform these athletic experiments without the emotional noise of criticism. As in any science, the work goes best when the experimenters fix their attention on the laboratory bench rather than on their opinions of themselves and each other.

The sun has disappeared and the river is dark. We round the last bend before Newell and are stunned at what confronts us. The entire Boston skyline is pitch black; the city has gone down, lights out. Only two ribbons of white, from car headlights streaming along the two riverbank roads, indicate life. The traffic looks heavy. Those headlights seem densely packed together, as if an evacuation were in progress. While we were upstream, did a nuclear war begin? In the boat we had left civilization behind, but we expected it to be there when we returned.

Later we learn what has happened. While we were rowing upstream tonight, November 9, 1965, the largest power outage in history occurred. It will come to be called the Great Northeast Blackout. At 5:16 P.M., a single transmission line in Niagara Falls, New York, failed, triggering a cascade of crashes in other power systems. Within five minutes, the electrical eclipse covered New York, Ontario, most of New England, and parts of New Jersey and Pennsylvania. The massive blackout left thirty million people without electricity for as long as thirteen hours.

But on the river we know nothing of this; on the river we have only darkness and our questions. Washburn tells us to *weigh enough,* and as the two boats stop and float midstream in front of Newell, Ted cautiously navigates his motor launch to its mooring and carries his megaphone out onto the dock. Peering through the gloom, he talks the coxswains in for our landings. He tells me to have my starboard side take three strokes, then hold water. *"All eight to row — ready all, row. . . . Weigh 'nough." "Starboards to row, ports to back, three strokes. Weigh 'nough."* And so on, much like an air traffic controller "talking down" a pilot whose instruments have quit.

Tonight we are not flying blind but rowing blind, in our coach's hands. Perhaps to some degree it is always thus. The dock looms into view. We land safely, quietly. Hushed, in a state of wonderment, we get out of the boat, remove the oars from the oarlocks, carry the shell into Newell, and, guided by flashlights, place it in its berth. I began this row feeling out of control, unable to stabilize my boat; by the end of our trip I could not see where I was going, nor was I even choosing my own words, instead functioning as a human megaphone relaying Ted's commands. An overloaded transmission line in Niagara Falls, New York, erased any lingering illusions I may have held about being in charge on the river. Yet I was not adrift. Nor was I afloat alone, and that was enough to bring my crew, and its passenger in the sternmost seat, safely to shore.

Perhaps it is simply fear of the dark, which grips even babies, or it may be dread of a less forgiving darkness: whatever the reason, on the river, we rowers instantly become anxious when the cox tells us to close our eyes. With vision shut down we feel vulnerable, less in control. *Something could happen.*

From a distance, rowing looks like a simple motion, but there is actually a great deal going on during each stroke. So much can go wrong: certain errors slow the boat imperceptibly, others can catapult a rower into the water. To row without sight feels like opening the door to ambush by floating guerrillas; everywhere they lie, scouting us, awaiting our lapse of vigilance.

Yet rowing without sight rebalances our sensory inputs in a useful way, opening new horizons. This is why the eyes-closed drill is a standard coaching tool. In darkness we discover how the boat sounds and feels. At the beginning of the stroke (called the *catch*, since that is when the oarblades first "catch" the water) we listen for a clean *plash* — identical and synchronized on port and starboard — as the oars, properly squared up, drop into the water. This sonority pleases a rower's ears just as the throaty *thwock* of a tennis ball on a racquet's sweet spot delights a tennis player. At the end of the stroke (the *release,* when the blades emerge from the water and "release" the boat to run forward), we listen for a quiet, crisp sort of suction, like the tearing of a fresh lettuce leaf.

In crews of two, four, or eight rowers, the sonorities of our blades mingle with those of our crewmates. Naturally, more oars make more sounds and hence perhaps obscure the source of a given note. This is the nature of social life. A solo cellist can sound fine playing alone, provided the instrument's strings are in tune with one another. But to play a duet or with an orchestra, the cellist must first "tune up" with fellow musicians to forge a common reference point. In a single scull we tune no blades but our own. But on a crew, the goal is not perfection of the individual but of the team, and so we seek unity and harmony.

Precise timing is essential: if eight oars strike the water even fractions of a second apart, they jerk the boat ahead unevenly, like cylinders misfiring in a V-8 engine. A rower whose blade enters the water even a fraction of a second late has momentarily reduced the crew from an eight to a seven. At the catch, the rowers strike their greatest blow against entropy, and whoever is late immediately becomes a form of ballast rather than a driving force: the shell is now surging ahead, and the late oar is going along for the ride. Imagine that eight men are about to lift a small automobile off the ground: each man hunkers down, grips the frame, and readies himself to lift up on the count of three. Whoever lifts a fraction of a second late may as well not be lifting at all; the task is already accomplished.

Rhythm, a rocking rhythm, a steady rhythm, is crucial. In crews we listen to the tone and texture of catches and releases and also for their *synchrony*, a key element in speed. When strokes synchronize perfectly, the crew pulls in phase, like light waves in a laser beam, and, as with a laser, the energies reinforce each other and multiply. To the crew, an eight-oared boat in peak form feels rowed by a single oar, and in a sense it is. The rowers' unifying awareness has come to life, and the shell stirs with it.

Even more important than sound is the feel of the boat. With eyes closed, we quickly sense the subtlest tilt to port or starboard. The shell runs smoothly under us or jerks ahead in jagged, sawtoothed progress. At the catch, we feel the oars grabbing the water, accelerating the boat instantly — or we sense the soft, slushy feeling of oars slipping through the water without bite.

Most of the power in the rowing stroke comes from the leg drive, because rowers sit on sliding seats that roll on wheels set in tracks. The sliding seat allows the rower's body to compress itself at the catch, as the legs bend nearly vertical. During the leg drive, the rower pushes the knees downward and straightens the legs, thus driving the sliding seat back and drawing the oar through the water. Then, after raising the oar out of the water, we glide up to the catch — toward the stern — and prepare another stroke. The trick is to execute this *recovery* phase of the stroke without reversing the shell's momentum. We can feel *checks* (hitches — stops — in the boat's forward motion) when rowers slide their weight too quickly toward the stern on the recovery. In darkness we learn what our crewmates are doing, since their every action touches our feelings through the medium of the boat.

In a rowing club, I once rowed behind a stroke who was an unusual oarsman in two ways: he was Chinese-American and he was blind. Every afternoon, a black Labrador Seeing Eye dog led Lee Chang down the dock to his place in the stroke seat. Lee was a strong and steady oarsman, a good stroke for our club eight. Stroking also minimized his chances of slamming into the rower in front of him (since there was none) in the event of a mishap, such as someone losing control of an oar and ceasing to row. Lee had a superb sense of the boat, his oar, and his crew; he merely guided himself by sound and feeling, rather than sight. Sighted or not, each of us ultimately reckons by our own inner compass. This poses no problem as long as the oarblades all arrive at the catch at the same instant.

There are sports that blind athletes could never attempt: baseball, basketball, soccer, lacrosse. These games involve interacting with moving objects and so demand vision; a blind person could as soon play tennis as drive a car. But a blind shot-putter or a discus or javelin thrower might throw as far as a sighted one. And consider running, swimming, skiing, rowing — in these endeavors blind athletes can perform well if they have a sighted ally to steer. Lee Chang could never have rowed a single scull, but he was a fine stroke for an eight, where the cox could be his eyes.

In this world we collide with those things that are invisible to us unless we have an ally who sees what we are blind to. The fatal condition is to be both blind and alone.

Whether our eyes have been closed by ourselves or by God, rowing in blindness simply amplifies a basic fact of life in shells: you don't see where you are going. Like all boats, racing shells progress in the direction of their bows. But rowers sit facing astern. Rowed boats differ from paddled boats, like canoes and kayaks — where the paddlers face their fate — in that racing shells have oarlocks and outriggers, which provide the fulcrum of the stroke. To use that leverage, the rower's back must be turned toward the bow while the rower faces the stern and the boat's wake. In this sense, we are all rowing blind.

In a single scull you are alone in the boat, so you must both row and steer. With two or four rowers, the one closest to the bow steers, by calling for harder strokes on port or starboard and with a kind of inboard tiller (called the "toe"), which responds to sideways movements of the foot. There are both coxed and uncoxed ("straight") pairs and fours. (One nickname for an uncoxed four is a "blind" four.) But all eight-oared boats have coxswains: these shells are so big, so fast, and turn so slowly that they would founder without a steersman.

You cannot steer completely by sound nor by the feel of the boat; somehow you must see what is ahead of you while facing astern. There are three ways to do this. The first and least common is a rearview mirror attached to an elastic headband. This is popular with older scullers, whose ability to rotate their necks may be limited. The second way is to look back over one's shoulder every few strokes, the technique most single scullers favor. The third method is to use a coxswain. The steersman, whether sitting behind the crew in the stern or before it in the bow, always faces the future.

Thus a crew can delegate its sense of sight to its cox, the eyes of the boat. Ideally, the crew trusts the cox to set its course. This permits the rowers to focus on sounds and feelings and on the central task of powering the boat. Ironically, once the coxswain has set a steering point, if the boat is on course the cox cannot see the point, since eight tall athletes block the view over the bow. (To peer around them by leaning to one side is verboten; it would drastically throw off the boat's set.) Hence, one paradox of coxing is that the destination heaves into view only when you are off course. Staying on course limits your attention to the boat and its rowers, who are, after all, the motor that takes you there. The goal does not disclose itself until it is attained.

Life can only be understood backward, said Kierkegaard, but unfortunately it must be lived forward. We never know what we are getting into, and only afterward do we understand where we have been. This philosophical analysis applies quite directly to the single scull, which allows a rower to steer forward while looking behind.

If you align the bow of your single with a desired point, you can then line up the tip of your stern with a landmark on shore, and the two points will determine a course. Then keep your stern on the shore point, make sure that your wake is straight, and you will be on course. The immediate past guides you into the future.

This technique is fine on a body of water that permits a long, straight trajectory. But a twisting river like the Charles requires a curvilinear course. Each major turn in the river means resetting one's steering point; to row straight ahead, navigating to an unchanging point off your stern will eventually run the boat aground. This is the classic difficulty with predicting the future from straight-line projections of the past. The river turns, conditions change, and we must respond by altering our course. There is no invariant formula for success. In fact, society and commerce also flow along serpentine paths, and those who miss their bends will, before long, find themselves grounded on the banks.

Although Storrow Drive, a major artery in Boston, winds alongside the Charles River, steering a car on Storrow Drive differs markedly from steering a shell on the Charles. A road has lanes and a direction; it funnels you to your destination: into Boston or away from it. A road has a fixed width; on Storrow Drive you'll travel the same distance as everyone else taking the same route. In contrast, the Charles widens and narrows, so the sculler who follows the riverbank will travel much farther than the one who shoots up the middle of the stream. The rower must navigate. In a car you have only to aim the front bumper and follow it home.

Consequently, driving a car is an "other-directed" activity. Drivers conform to a course laid out by others — engineers, politicians, and paving contractors. Sometimes the road that dictates their course was built centuries earlier; the story goes that traffic in downtown Boston essentially follows cowpaths originally worn in by seventeenth-century cattle. Road travelers do not blaze new trails. But to row, you have to cut your own path through the water. There is no template. Each time out on the river means finding a fresh route to your destination.

A few conventions govern boat traffic on the Charles. The most important one by far is that upstream travelers stay to the "Cambridge" side, while downstream traffic keeps to the "Boston" side. These two cities face each other across the river, with Cambridge, roughly speaking, on the northern/western bank and Boston on the southern/eastern one. The rule, devised to prevent collisions, imposes some order on the flow of river traffic. Since rowers spend most of their time facing backward, observing this custom is most important.

But there are no lane markers on the water's surface, so the knotty question becomes: how far over should you stay? There is a no-man's-land in the center of the river, not clearly on either side. Furthermore, this midstream water is generally the most desirable place to row, because it permits the straightest course: by shooting up the middle of the Charles, we can remove the kinks from the river. Staying close to the riverbank puts us on a meandering route.

The outer course is the more cautious route, favored by beginners. The center of the action is, inevitably, the arena of jeopardy.
By staying away from the mainstream we can avoid most of the
traffic, especially the hazardous traffic coming the other way. Yet
the river's edge has its own snares: overhanging tree branches,
shallow water, submerged sandbars. In general, the hazards of the
marginal course are fixed while those of the mainstream (other
boats) are in motion; rowing in the middle of the river requires a
higher degree of alertness. As a single sculler gains skill, the act of
rowing the boat does not occupy the mind so completely, so we can
devote more attention to steering. Mastery lets us dare that faster,
riskier course up the middle. It is another way in which we trade
security for speed.

Although steering requires vision, sight is secondary; an experienced cox steers mostly by feeling, by kinesthesia. The hull of a
rowing shell is only one-sixteenth of an inch thick or even thinner;
it is a skin, a membrane through which the coxswain senses the
river and its response to the boat. The water talks to the coxswain
through the hull. Through specific touch points — backside on
the seat, feet on the hull, hands on the rudder ropes — the steersman *feels*. The river rushes along both sides of the hull and beneath
it; any shift in the set, pitch, or heading of the boat reaches the cox
instantly. The coxswain reflexively balances these inputs with tiny
adjustments of the rudder, tweaks that precede thought. Reason is
too blunt a tool for steering; you steer an eight by instinct. It is like
riding the back of a sixty-foot ski, which you can gracefully turn
either way, or keep to a straight course, merely by putting pressure
on one edge or another.

Some years ago I learned to sail small boats in the Charles River
Basin. One sunny Saturday afternoon, on a minimalist boat called

a Laser, I experienced a sailing satori, a moment of revelation that dissolved the boundary between myself and my surroundings. The line in my left hand controlled the sail, and it felt as if I held the wind in my hand, of which the sail surface was only an extension. My right hand held the rudder, plunged underwater, where I could feel the water so intimately that the rudder might have been my palm. I became simply a pivot linking wind and water; my task was to sense these two elements and mediate between them. No thinking was needed — in fact, thoughts would have hindered me. Suddenly "I" vanished and instead there was a unified field of water, wind, and a translator in their conversation; what is more, this translator was conscious, and hence could steer. The rest of the day was ecstasy. That was the afternoon I learned to sail, and also discovered something about steering. To steer does not mean imposing your will on your surroundings, but rather being so fully in touch with the proximate forces that, almost without effort, you enlist them in your chosen course. On the best days, there may be only a trifling difference between steering and being steered, perhaps no more than an inner conviction about where to go.

Looking ahead, a coxswain finds a *point,* a landmark of some kind on the shore to use as a lodestar. On any voyage we need a fixed object to orient us — whether it be Polaris, a lighthouse, or the happiness of our family. Without a point to steer to, our destination changes with our position, and this verges perilously close to *drifting.* A drifter is someone who is blown to a different course by every circumstance or whim of fate, one who has no direction in life. There are indeed many pointless lives.

In contrast, a steersman takes charge of life's course, targets actions toward an end that endures, knows the destination and keeps it in view. The steersman holds to a meaningful purpose. An unswerving commitment does not, however, mean an unswerving course. A jetliner flying from Los Angeles to Hawaii, after a trip of twenty-five hundred miles, lands on a Honolulu runway within a few feet of its targeted end point. *Yet for 99 percent of the voyage the plane has been off course:* at virtually every moment of the flight, it deviated to some degree from the optimal heading for Honolulu. But a constant stream of small corrections by the autopilot, and by the human pilots, took the jet precisely to its destination.

It is not necessary to be perfect; we can make thousands of mistakes during our voyage. What is required is that we commit ourselves to a course and remain alert to the actualities of each moment, so we can guide our adjustments. While steering a course, the cox continuously responds to circumstances — wind, current, and the temperament of the crew, for example — reacting to these momentary conditions while aiming at a settled target. To engage oneself in this way is to grasp the tiller, to take charge of the direction in which we travel, and ultimately, to reach our desired ends. At every moment we have a choice: to drift or to steer.

I had heard of Harvard's varsity rowing coach before I entered college. Five days after I graduated from high school in June of 1965, for the first and only time, a college crew and their coach appeared on the cover of *Sports Illustrated.* "Harvard Coach Harry Parker and the World's Best Crew" ran the headline; Parker was then only twenty-nine years old but had already become an invincible force in college rowing.

When head coach Harvey Love died of a heart attack in January 1963, Harry Parker suddenly became Harvard's varsity coach. That spring, coaching Ted Washburn's crew, he immediately showed a talent for making fast boats; Harvard won three races and lost one. In June, Harvard upset Yale by an astounding eight boat lengths, and from that point on Harvard would not lose a regular-season crew race until 1969, reeling off five consecutive undefeated sea-

sons from 1964 through 1968. They would win eighteen consecutive Yale races, not losing until 1981.

In the fall of 1965, Parker was at the peak of his *Wunderkind*
phase; he reigned as a Delphic oracle, a recondite genius of the
sport. Every day, as my freshman crew trained at Newell Boathouse, his aura infused the air, and we inhaled it. Over the following years, I made an extended study of the Parker magic; there was
much to learn from Harry, who became the dominant American
rowing coach of the second half of the twentieth century, and
perhaps of all time. I often pondered the question that most of the
rowing world was puzzling over: what is Harry's secret?

There is no single answer to this riddle; Harry is a complex man
who does many things well, and part of his genius is that he does
not coach by formula. The coach who enshrines a system for
winning stops learning new ways to win. Harry, however, does not
stop learning; even now, long after he has reached a level of ac-
knowledged mastery, he tries something new every year. The annual turnover of athletes in a college crew asks this of any coach
with high aspirations: each year's crop needs its own brand of
coaching. Harry has won with big oarsmen and relatively small
ones, with technically polished crews and with hammers, with star
athletes and without them, with hippies and preppies, showboats
and yuppies.

Parker's goal has not changed over the years: to build the fastest
possible varsity boat and to take it to the highest level of competition it can reach — the national championship, the World Championships, even, in some years, the Olympic Games. (One of
Parker's varsity crews was the last college eight to represent the
United States in the Olympics, at Mexico City in 1968.) But while
his target remains fixed, each year he must find a new path toward
that goal.

Coaches are also steersmen, in part because they are educators.

Many of Harry's athletes identify him as the best and most important teacher they had at Harvard. The words *educate* and *educe* stem from the same root: the Latin *educere*, to lead forth. Real education does not install knowledge in the brain; rather, it evokes potentials that exist in the student, developing innate talents and abilities. The coach does not impose goals on the crew, but serves as an external agent who enables the crew to realize the ambitions they already hold. The coach leads the athletes forth.

In 1948, the mathematician and philosopher Norbert Wiener coined the word *cybernetic*, from the Greek *kubermetes*, meaning "governor" or "steersman." Wiener noted that living systems have built-in processes of control and communication — feedback loops that regulate their overall functioning toward certain ends. For example, when a bone breaks, the human body marshals a biochemical response to the damage through the bloodstream; repair and rebuilding of the bone commence immediately, and over a period of weeks, the infinitely complex process regulates and completes itself. As the bone returns to normal, waning biochemical signals from the site gradually shut down the rebuilding process. The body does not continue to build bone after the restoration is complete; informational feedback governs the healing response.

Another, more homely example of feedback is the thermostat, which turns on the furnace when the indoor temperature falls below, say, 68 degrees Fahrenheit. When the temperature reaches 68 degrees, the thermostat senses this and shuts the furnace off.

Similarly, a coach and crew form a cybernetic system, a feedback loop. The coach continually senses the pulse of the crew in order to know what this particular crew needs to do right now. It could mean working harder or taking a day off, long endurance pieces or technical drills, rowing with eyes closed or racing against the junior varsity on rough water in a boat so poorly rigged that the varsity is sure to lose. The coach notices current reality and then intervenes, designing actions to bring about a desired outcome — like winning a big regatta or even the national championship.

Like any worthwhile endeavor, winning is difficult. Valleys of discouragement and doubt interpose themselves between desire and fulfillment, between wanting a gold medal and wearing one. To continue moving forward despite setbacks, the crew needs a coach who not only monitors and responds to their state but holds their highest ambitions constant, despite the most disruptive surprises and problems. They need, in short, a coach who is a *willful character*.

Harry Parker is such a character. He does not allow hindrances to thwart the attainment of his desire; *he will not be denied.* In playing any game with Harry, whether it be horseshoes, croquet, Monopoly, or soccer, the upper limit to the competition will always be set by his opponent; there is no point at which Harry will say, "This isn't worth it." Parker is someone who will go to the end of the line to get what he wants. A willful character stops at nothing.

Someone's response to obstacles reveals who they are, what they actually value. Is it comfort? Then they will reset their priorities when the situation gets uncomfortable. In Harry's case, when something comes between him and his goal, he finds a way to handle the problem: going over it, going around it, or perhaps just mowing it down. Resourcefulness conquers all.

For example, when I was in college, the University of Pennsylvania was Harvard's archrival in rowing. Parker himself is a Penn alumnus who had learned to row at Penn, and his cherished coach and mentor, Joe Burk, still headed the Penn crew. Thus, beating Penn in the annual Adams Cup regatta, which pitted Harvard against Penn and Navy, was especially meaningful. Harvard's crew enjoyed that satisfaction for five years running, but in the spring of 1969 Penn won the cup, finishing almost two boat lengths ahead of

Harvard and thus snapping the undefeated streak that stretched back to 1963. A week later, Parker and Harvard avenged the loss by beating Penn at the Eastern Sprints.

After the 1969 season, Burk retired as Penn's coach. His successor, Penn's freshman coach, Ted Nash, had by then become an almost satanic figure in the minds of Harvard oarsmen, mostly due to an accretion of undergraduate mythology. During the 1960s, as opposing freshman coaches, Nash and Washburn were intense rivals. Washburn's Harvard freshmen won the Eastern Sprints in 1965 and 1967, and Nash's Penn frosh prevailed in 1966, 1968, and 1969. Nash is a larger-than-life figure, a charismatic coach who invents inspiring slogans and shibboleths for his athletes to rally around. His over-the-top style contrasts with Parker's taciturn, intense demeanor, a product of the restrained New England tradition.

In 1970, when Nash became head coach at Penn, he faced not Ted Washburn's freshmen but Harry Parker's varsity. In that year's Adams Cup regatta, Penn beat Harvard by more than a boat length, a devastating loss. Emotionally, most coaches would need at least a day to recover from such a defeat before going back to the drawing board. But moments after the finish, in the coaches' launch, Parker and Washburn were already analyzing the weak and strong points of the race, calmly figuring out ways to beat Penn the next time around. One week later, Harvard won the Eastern Sprints, beating Penn by half a length.

On the heels of that Adams Cup defeat, Parker focused on his crew's future success rather than his own emotional reactions to the loss. Harry's persistent, riveting attention reflects his phenomenal engagement with the task. His is an artistic temperament, ruled by a compelling focus on what he is creating; ride with Harry in his launch during a workout and you will not end up having a light conversation; back in the boathouse, you will rarely see him sitting around batting the breeze with the other coaches. To Parker, the loss to Penn was simply another challenge, another test, a difficult turn in the varsity's voyage. Undeniably it was an opportunity to learn, one that Harvard could ignore only at its peril.

Harvard rowers generally bring their own willfulness to the boathouse; Parker's example may strengthen what they already have. Sometimes Harry gives them more direct counsel. For example, inevitably there are times during a race when the oarsmen feel they have reached their limit: burning quadriceps are screaming, *No more.* There is a phrase Parker sometimes uses for such moments of truth: *Don't take No for an answer.* That phrase — *Don't take No for an answer* — neatly defines a willful character.

A willful character's fuel may be desire that burns with exceptional intensity. Such compelling desire — whether it be to win a regatta, to create a unique sculpture, or to discover a secret of the natural world — can function as a kind of magnetic north, reliably guiding one's inner compass. Desire, amid shifting winds and currents, can project a polestar into the heavens.

Not long after our extraordinary row on the night of the blackout, my freshman crew completed its fall rowing season, and it was time to go indoors to the tanks for the winter. When the Charles River freezes, the tanks are an excellent way to simulate a workout on the water. Only a handful of American college crews have the luxury of indoor tanks, and Harvard is one of them. The setup resembles the inside of a rowing shell — a boat, stripped of its hull, sunk into concrete. There are eight sliding seats, foot stretchers that hold the rowers' feet in place, outriggers, oarlocks, and oars. Long shallow pools of water, deep enough to cover a squared oarblade, flank the port and starboard sides of the "boat." A diesel engine in the bowels of Newell drives a pump that can channel water through the pools, simulating a river current as well as the motion of the "boat" relative to water.

Not only do the oarsmen build rowing-specific musculature and endurance in the tanks, but the setup allows coaches to observe each athlete's technique at close range and to correct errors with a kind of individual attention that is nearly impossible on the water.

These winter workouts are also a learning opportunity for coxswains. It is a chance to see the athletes row together every day and to learn each oarsman's idiosyncrasies from a vantage point not available on the water. The indoor coaching sessions inundate the cox with knowledge about rowing technique. And simply by showing up for the unglamorous tank sessions in Newell, the cox builds a bond with the crew. *He is there for us.*

There is, however, little for a cox to do in the tanks. No boat ride, no course to steer nor rudder to set, no need to balance the shell, and precious few orders to give. The winter is a coxswain's ordeal, a test of commitment. It is not a trial by fire nor even of water. It is a trial by boredom.

Unfortunately, my boredom threshold is low, and the tanks were my undoing. Three winter months cooped up in the dank concrete tank room seemed more than I could endure. Coxing in the fall had indeed presented me with challenges and exotic skills to learn. Since we had not raced, I had no idea of how I might fare competitively, nor how my talents compared with those of the other boys trying out for coxswain. But the level of physical activity in coxing, even on the river, was too low for my taste; while the oarsmen heated up with an intense workout, I was confined to sitting still — *very* still — on a narrow wooden seat. Burning no calories, I was cold out there on the river on a windy fall day. The glories of crew had not reached deeply enough into me to pull me through that winter of discontent.

Academic life also worried me. Throughout high school, like most of my classmates, I had rarely seen a grade other than A on my report card. But the academics at Harvard College were rich fuel, of considerably higher octane than I had been used to at

Dover High School. It seemed, for example, that I had run out of talent in mathematics. Having breezed through my high school math courses with straight As, as a college freshman I stared, clueless, for long hours at theorem proofs in integral calculus. Only by dint of hammer-and-tongs studying did I manage to pull out a C+ in the course. Today such a mark would be tantamount to failing, but in 1965 it was actually a respectable, if not distinguished, grade. Nonetheless it came as a shock to my system. In my fall semester I attained only one A−, in freshman composition, while achieving lackluster grades in my other courses.

Thus, for the first time, sports and studies came into conflict. I was unlikely to flunk out of Harvard, but my fall term transcript certainly questioned my ability to ace the academic side of life. If academics were my bread-and-butter, my arena of mastery, could I risk losing my edge there? Did other involvements, like crew, sap energy from my courses? Had I burned with a passion to cox, the conflict would have been a trying one. But under the circumstances, the winning move was clear: to put my chips on the number that had come up for me.

Thus did my foray into intercollegiate athletics come to an end. That winter I left Harvard's freshman crew and in the spring learned to play squash, which took less time and offered scheduling flexibility. My grades did not instantly improve. However, I survived freshman year and as a sophomore began earning As and Bs, eventually graduating *magna cum laude*. I relished those heady college years; Harvard in the late 1960s was an unforgettable experience. But I never went out for another varsity sport.

Sometimes I wonder how my life might have been different had I stuck out those tank sessions and gone on to cox the freshman crew in the spring. My erstwhile teammates who made the first freshman boat had a good season, winning three races and losing only one, to Penn. They placed second at the Eastern Sprints, again behind Penn. At the end of the year they beat Yale. Cleve Livingston and Fritz Hobbs, two of the beginners in my rocky boat on the night of the Great Northeast Blackout, were future world-class athletes; both rowed in the United States eight at the Mexico City Olympics and won silver medals at the Munich Games in 1972. Their coach on those Olympic crews was Harry Parker.

Had I continued as a cox, perhaps I might have steered Harvard's varsity eight as an upperclassman. I might even have gone to the Olympics with Cleve and Fritz. Who knows? If only I had been steering, they — we — might even have won the gold at Munich . . .

Or, perhaps, only the bronze. In any case these are idle dreams, unlikely for many reasons, including the fact that during college I outgrew the coxswain's seat. I was a late bloomer; my physical growth continued until age twenty, and by graduation I stood 5 feet 7 inches tall and weighed 145 pounds. To get down to coxing weight would have been very difficult, if not impossible.

So I missed out on no Olympic medals by quitting freshman crew. What I did lose was an unusual chance to test myself in a rarefied athletic world. *You cannot step twice into the same river,* said Heraclitus, *for other waters are ever flowing on to you.* Throughout college and afterward, rowing continued to fascinate me. I went to regattas and made some lifelong friends on Harvard's varsity boats. However, many years would pass before I again shoved off from a dock, feeling that familiar floating anxiety, but this time in another seat, in another boat; by then I would be launching from a different point on the river, and steering a different course.

Equinox

To be on the wire is life; the rest is waiting.

— KARL WALLENDA, aerialist

THE QUALITY OF BALANCE is fundamental not only to boats, but to the solar system. Since the axis of this planet tilts, skewing our attitude toward the sun, our terrestrial climate varies throughout the year. As Earth circles its star in annual orbit, sunlight gradually inflects its angle and duration. Hence the four seasons. Twice a year, the hours of daylight and darkness equal each other, at the vernal and autumnal equinoxes, the year's two moments of balance between sun and shadow.

The word *equinox* combines the Latin *equi* (equal) and *nox* (night). *Equal night.* A counterpoise of light and darkness. Right/ wrong, black/white, day/night. The equinox is a symmetry between sun and shadow: weigh them out, as if trays suspended from Libra, the equal-arm balance scale of the Romans, held these solar energies. *Libra* names the zodiacal sign (also called Scales or Balance) that begins on the autumnal equinox, when the sun enters its constellation.

Still, sunlight and darkness are distinct qualities; they cannot really offset each other. It makes no sense to set them on opposite sides of an equals sign; they are as different as night and day. Yet in another way it does make sense to oppose them, since they share the same continuum: darkness is simply the absence of light. Starting at dawn, the day gradually increases its illumination and then recedes from full radiance. There is no perfect blackness; stars pierce the midnight sky. Nor is there, as far as we can see, any ultimate light.

In the boats we have to find countless balances. The shell itself is a kind of scale, with oars for arms. Steering, for example, requires balance: the forces on port and starboard must match each other for the shell to go straight; otherwise, it veers to the weak side. Sculling in a single, a curving wake tells you that you are stronger on one side than the other. In a pair, the two rowers must be of comparable size and strength, else one will constantly "pull the other around," as the phrase goes. In any two-person team, persistent imbalance results in dominance, and generally this is undesirable, whether in rowing, business partnerships, or marriages. On larger crews, like fours, you might hear a rower say, "The starboards were pulling the ports around," a form of good-natured ribbing seasoned with a boast: *we starboards overpowered you ports.* But in more serious moments the crew knows that if true, this is not good news. When making up their boatings, coaches must consider, among all the other factors, an equal distribution of power.

Equality appears in the image of blind justice, the blindfolded goddess holding a balance scale. In our collective life we also seek equilibrium. For example, democratic governments have long struggled to balance the ideals of freedom and equality. Unfortunately, we cannot maximize both at once, since they are intrinsically incompatible. To enforce universal equality means sharply restricting personal freedom: every communist government, for example, has been, by necessity, totalitarian. Conversely, total free-

dom, as under laissez-faire capitalism, results in vast social dispari-
ties — and, ironically, a loss of freedom for those at the bottom of
the pyramid.

If we turn to nature a different picture emerges. The natural
world embodies a condition that could be called "freedom," but
calling it that imposes a human concept onto something more
basic. Even more foreign to nature is the concept of equality, which
is meaningless in the natural world, where nothing equals anything
else: each plant and animal is unique. Equality is a human idea that
only human institutions attempt to enforce.

Instead of equality, nature strives for balance. In a balanced,
complex ecosystem like a deciduous forest or an ocean cove, each
life form expresses itself to its fullest capacity within the con-
straints of the biological community. Other plants and animals —
and elements like sea water and loam — limit the dominance of
any one species. Each organism has its niche. Relationships among
these different forms of life continuously reconfigure, creating the
dynamic equilibrium of ecological balance. This harmonious state
constantly encounters shifting conditions and new challenges, and
thus the living community optimizes the speed of its evolution.

While there is no real alternative to "freedom" in nature, there is
a condition that mimes totalitarianism. This is monoculture: the
dominance of a plant habitat by a single species, just as a single
philosophy dominates totalitarian society. Monocultures are simple — a huge farm growing nothing but durum wheat; a lawn with
only fescue grass; a wetland taken over by an exotic invader like
purple loosestrife. Like equality, monocultures are a human arti-
fact, nearly always the result of human intervention.

The opposite of a monoculture is a tropical rain forest, an
infinitely complex ecosystem with hundreds of thousands of inter-
dependent species that has taken millions of years to evolve such
diversity and strength. A rain forest is a resilient ecosystem: if one

species fades or disappears, the immensely diverse biological community responds to restore the natural balance. In contrast, a monoculture is vulnerable to extermination: a pest or drought that destroys the tyrannical species erases the entire vegetative substrate and sets the evolutionary clock back eons. Monolithic concepts, whether in agriculture or philosophy, invite disaster. Complex relatedness enhances resilience and thereby adds survival value.

Similar patterns apply to the human body, whose internal ecology is as complex as that of a rain forest. A healthy body keeps itself in equilibrium: millions of biochemical feedback loops closely regulate things like uptake of oxygen, blood glucose level, and body temperature. Persistent imbalance eventually results in disease.

Balance, then, is not mere parity of amounts, even if the scales of Libra settle level. There is balance in an abstract painting when a burning coal of red in the lower left corner offsets a sprawling cobalt-blue whorl diagonally opposite. The shining sonority of an alto saxophone can balance a moody piano line and the rich musings of a string bass. There can be balance in a menu for Saturday's lunch: cheese soufflé, salad vinaigrette, flinty Chardonnay, crusty bread. Balance is neither neutral nor homogeneous: it often holds sharp, primal elements in equilibrium. On the water, even as the rowers unleash terrific forces, the port and starboard oars, with great delicacy, keep the boat poised.

Next to love, balance is the most important thing, said John Wooden, the legendary UCLA basketball coach. In sports, balance is the foundation of everything else. In basketball, sound footwork, resulting in a balanced distribution of weight, allows us to hit a jump shot, to deter a charge down the foul lane, to block out an opponent and control the boards.

In soccer there is a maxim: *if you don't have possession, get position.* The defender who is better positioned and better balanced than the attacker will likely win the ball. Football running backs who keep their center of gravity low, their feet near the ground, are difficult to tackle. The stability of the lower body allows precise kicks and also enables upper-body moves such as swinging a tennis racquet and throwing a discus — or a left jab. In crew, a balanced shell is the platform that provides a steady fulcrum for the oars. Any scale needs a level foundation: if the floor is tilted, the arms of Libra tilt with it and prevent an accurate weighing. On the water, instability is fatal: a pitching, tilting shell is impossible to row well.

Women's gymnastics makes it explicit: one event is called the balance beam. On that beam, four inches wide and nearly four feet above the floor, imbalance is catastrophic, resulting, quite literally, in a fall from grace. *Balance is poise.* In sports, as elsewhere, what we do is secondary to the posture from which we do it. Any action will be effective if executed with poise. In fencing, for example, the power of a thrust depends on the soundness of the fencer's footing. In a business setting, a negotiating posture that combines flexibility with a willingness to decline any given deal often proves forceful. In personal relations, our underlying motives — our *posture* — generally matters more than our specific behavior. For example, any words or deeds that arise from real love will tend to connect us with others.

However, balance is no settled state: it is alive, dynamic, constantly emergent. Even those ideal moments when our boat sets up perfectly, flying across the water in silent, level splendor, only mean balance *now.* A second later, we must take the next stroke.

In rowing, as in life, there are countless factors to balance, not merely port and starboard. We need to counterpoise power and technique, teamwork and individuality, confidence and uncertainty. Balance is a recipe that combines ingredients into something whole. This may include symmetry, or it may offset symmetrical elements against asymmetrical ones. Balance finds integrity, creating unity within even the most dazzling oppositions of vivid colors or natural forces.

Speed demands that we risk our balance. Velocity comes with volatility. The faster the boat, the more provisional its set. On expert ski trails, racing bicycles, and high-performance figure skates, faster means lighter, racier, more agile, streamlined. In contrast, security demands clunky supports that stabilize the structure, even as they sap us of speed. That which is stable is slow.

Nonetheless, stable, slow platforms help beginners learn a new skill without worrying about balance. We progress from tricycles to training wheels, then to two-wheelers. The need for stable equipment disappears as our capacity for balance grows: as our inner gyroscope takes over the balancing act, we can remove the external supports.

With increasing skill, we learn to move boats faster, and the laws of physics help solve the balance problem. A shell has a small fin, about the size of an index card, on its hull. The pressure of water against the fin — on an airplane wing this force would be called *lift* — damps the shell's tendency to roll from side to side. This pressure increases with the *square* of the shell's forward velocity. So although fast boats are volatile, fast rowers collect the dividend of speed: greatly increased stability. On the river, as on Wall Street, the rich get richer.

Single sculls, with only two oars and a crew of one, distill the elements of the balance problem. A single sculler starts in a wherry, a heavy craft with a wide, flat-bottomed hull, like a slender rowboat with outriggers and a sliding seat. The wherry sets up easily and so makes an ideal platform for learning the basics of sculling. These fundamentals include learning how to grip the oars —

lightly, with knuckles over the front of the handle, thumbs against the tips. Each oar has a collar, known as the button, which the sculler keeps pressed against the oarlocks; this sets a stable fulcrum for the oar's leverage. The position of the button on the shaft also determines how much of the shaft will be inboard; in other words, where that fulcrum will be relative to the entire length of the oar. The beginner also learns that during the stroke, the left hand passes above the right, and that to keep the shell balanced, one must keep both hands at nearly the same height.

As skill grows, the neophyte progresses to an intermediate shell, lighter and less stable, and then to a racing single — even lighter and even more volatile. At the gossamer extreme, where boat designers flirt with the official rules, racing singles weigh about a pound per foot; a Van Dusen shell might approach the international minimum of 14 kilograms (about 31 pounds) — and in the past, Van Dusen has built singles as light as 22 pounds.

Twenty-six feet long with an 18-foot wingspan, the single scull is about triple the length and width of our own bodies, so we imagine the craft as enormous, ourselves its small passengers. This is an illusion. Forget size and consider weight: if we are rowing a 30-pound single with a 150-pound body, our own mass is five times that of the boat. Consequently, even minor physical quirks — for example, lowering the left shoulder at the catch — will drastically corrupt the boat's set.

Thus in the single, as everywhere, we tend to overlook our own effect on our experience. External realities — boats, oars, water, sky, wind — seem to dwarf our insignificant selves. Yet, consider an example quite close to home: the human head and neck can weigh 10–15 pounds. In a single, your head may weigh half as much as your boat. We must keep our heads poised and centered; otherwise, the boat instantly pitches to one side. Coaches criticize rowers for "sightseeing" — swiveling their heads to one side or the other — because even in an eight, tiny asymmetries play havoc with the set. When our attention strays, the boat's balance goes with it.

The shell responds to motions of the body. The body follows the dictates of the mind. Hence the boat reacts to the rower's mind: when your mind quivers, so does your shell. Thought waves toss the hull. Conversely, a quiet mind levels the boat; stillness settles the body, and the shell, relaxing into agreement, takes the quietest, fastest route through the water. A peaceful, poised environment has its source in consciousness that is peaceful and poised. We ourselves give our experience its dominant imprint and form: we are always at the center of the universe.

From high overhead, the July sunlight fans quicksilver across the river's surface; an undulating mirror atop blue liquid, it glitters, a sky facing upward. Any movement — a tilt of my head, perhaps even a shift in thought — alters the sparkling pattern. Wind rakes the water into trembling furrows. And we quiver too; inside the boat we are an arrow notched on a bowstring, pulled taut, ready to be let fly.

Yet the starter holds us back; the simplest things seem to take hours; he frets with the boats endlessly, aligning them — *Can't we just start this race and get it over with?* — as we throb for release; high tension charges the air like a live wire, an open circuit sputtering white sparks.

Soon I will row into pain. The hurt may pay off: winning would be sensational. Yet losing only redoubles the agony. Only one of these two states — and no other — awaits us at the finish line. These polar charges, this either/or, electrify this moment.

Since conflict fuels drama, perhaps to whet our appetites for life, we invent oppositions. Simplicity seduces the mind, splits life into positive and negative poles: *right/wrong, black/white, day/night.* And, of paramount importance: *win/lose.* Not all cultures keep score as ferociously as we do; Americans not only accent winning but worship it. The binary logic of computers, the on/off code of 0 and 1, is an all-American mode: in this country, you're either #1 or you're nothing. Winning even forms our sense of personal worth: to call someone a winner or a loser makes a statement about character. Of course we care about the scoreboard with unseemly passion. How could we not?

Consider the annual Harvard-Yale football game. Surely the spectators — mostly Harvard and Yale students, alumni, and families — include some of the most intelligent people in North America. At tailgate parties before the game, they share sophisticated food and conversation. But, entering the stadium for the contest, the same crowd may as well be filing into the Roman Colosseum to view gladiators. Nuanced observations give way to on/off responses: move the football ten yards in one direction, and the Harvard fans rise cheering while those from Yale deflate. Move it ten yards the other way and the reactions reverse themselves. These drastic mood swings often flip back and forth in seconds. Inside the stadium, the "best and the brightest" regress to Stone Age reflexes, ruled by hormones and the part of the brain that evolved first, the so-called reptilian brain.

Rooting for a team, we identify our survival with its fate: the players are our warriors, protectors, champions. The word *champion* roots itself in the Old English *cempa,* meaning "warrior," and the Latin *campus,* a level field, a place for military exercises and games, a field of battle. Cognates include *camp* and *campaign.* Though they know otherwise, spectators feel winning to be a matter of life or death. Nowadays the stakes are symbolic ones, but the reptilian brain does not distinguish the symbolic from the sanguinary. To the unconscious mind, imagined experiences are real.

Sports are a form of play. But they are also war games, civilized versions of combat. Throwing the javelin tests a soldier's ability to hurl a spear; football games mimic the clash of two armies over contested territory. As civilization has turned cavalry skirmishes into polo, moving competition from battlefield to playing field, the object has changed from killing the enemy to outscoring the opponents. But the feelings — *this is life or death* — persist. Sidelines, rules, and referees hardly matter to the adrenal cortex, the hormonal center that controls so many instincts and emotions.

At the ancient Greek Olympic Games there were no gold, silver, or bronze medals. There was only one winner, who wore the laurel wreath: *you were either #1, or you were nothing.* Then as now, to lose was devastating. At the end of the eighth Pythian Ode, the fifth-century B.C. poet Pindar describes those unlucky souls defeated at the games: "The others slink down back alleys, out of sight of their enemies, bitten by disaster."

The Hellenic Olympics staged no regattas. Ancient oarsmen rowed not for laurel wreaths but for blood, in savage wars governed only by the imperative of kill or be killed. Against seagoing enemies, rowing had military value. Free from dependence on wind, rowed boats could outmaneuver sailing boats, especially on calm days or amid unfriendly gusts. For civilians, they offered the same advantages as a form of transportation.

Ancient Phoenicia, Greece, and other Mediterranean nations built galleys propelled by one, two, or three banks of rowers, stacked vertically. During the Assyrian Empire (1700–600 B.C.), navies rowed the two-banked galleys called *biremes*, and three-tiered Greek *triremes* appeared around 650 B.C. (*Trireme* is actually a Latin word; the Greeks called them *trieres*.) A trireme might seat 170 oarsmen: two lower banks of 54 rowers each (27 ports, 27 starboards) and an upper bank of 62. The thunderous approach of such a battleship must have inspired awe, as its huge tiers of oars beat like wings; the ancients described the *trieres* as a bird of prey.

In naval warfare, the goal is simple: *get there before they do.* That, in a nutshell, is a regatta. Like all races, rowing contests repeat the struggle to stay alive. *We cannot let them catch us.*

With life and death at stake, naturally we are anxious at the starting line. Even so, other fears graze the mind. Several drastic mishaps can occur during a crew race; most are rare, but simply by lurking in the shallows, they add an uneasy backdrop to the start. The likeliest disaster, and hence the most troubling one, is *catching a crab.* Let us draw near this supremely mortifying event.

Imagine, then, an enormous wheel, a wheel of fortune or perhaps of the dharma; the essential thing is to know that whatever the wheel, it is you who turns it. For now, let it be a huge bicycle wheel, about twenty feet across, mounted on an axle in the floor so it can spin like a roulette wheel. Your job is to get this wheel turning as fast as possible using a long wooden paddle that you can insert between the spokes. Call this stick an oar. Pulling your oar turns the wheel — slowly at first, as it overrides inertia. Release the oar, let the wheel spin, then again plunge it into the whirling fan of spokes for another stroke.

To build speed, add seven teammates with oars, the eight of you spaced around the bicycle tire, which has a circumference of more than sixty feet. On each stroke all eight thrust their oars into the spokes at the same moment, propel the wheel for exactly the same distance, then pull the oars out precisely together. After a few such strokes, pulling as hard as you can each time, the big wheel hums along, revolving at a terrific rate. If the eight of you stay synchronized, you can keep this up indefinitely. Friction slows the wheel down just before each new stroke, which revives it with a fresh boost of energy. The longer, stronger, and more numerous your strokes and the better synchronized they are, the faster the wheel spins.

Now comes trouble. Suppose that on one stroke your seven

teammates extract their oars together, but you do not. You are a bit tardy, slightly late in removing your oar from the spokes, which are just now reaching their highest velocity from the fresh stroke. Imagine what happens next. First, your oar will be trapped, grabbed by the spokes, which have now spun past your release point. If you cling to your oar, its terrific momentum will manhandle you — lift you off your feet and perhaps heave you into the teammate directly behind or slam you somewhere else as it careens on its wayward course. The possessed oar will have its way, and *you cannot get it out of the spokes.* Or: let go of the handle, and the oar clobbers you with great force, perhaps slamming into your chest, shoulders, or neck. It feels a bit like being in the path of a baseball bat, swung hard. The wheel has exacted its revenge: you have met your fate, or, rather, it has met you. Perhaps it is, after all, a wheel of dharma.

The bicycle wheel is, of course, the water in which we row, and this mishap is called catching a crab. When you are late extracting your blade and it gets stuck underwater — as the boat surges ahead — it can indeed feel as if the claws of a giant blue crab, just below the surface, have seized your oar and held it fast. The momentum of an eight hurtling forward at full speed, leveraged onto a twelve-foot oar, can actually eject an oarsman from his seat, the shaft flicking him out of the shell like a grape on the tip of a teaspoon — or it can slam the oar handle into him with the impact of a diesel engine. Catching a crab is terrifying.

Yet it is essential to catch crabs: it is a rower's dharma. The Sanskrit word *dharma,* meaning "law," evokes both duty and destiny, the principle that orders the universe. It is our duty to catch crabs; they are an intrinsic part of the rower's learning process. The term *crab* actually refers to several acute problems that involve getting one's oar caught in the water, but the "late release" version just described is the classic beginner's error.

Like all mistakes, crabs come in several sizes. The monster crabs that eject rowers from boats are quite rare, but a good, whacking, "over the head" crab, which propels the oar handle above or even behind the athlete's head, shows up often enough in novice boats. There are also incomplete crabs, perhaps little more than snags at the release; they disrupt one's rhythm annoyingly without jerking the oar out of control; perhaps these should be called crayfish.

In this world, nothing is free. Every endeavor has its version of crabs; they are a form of paying dues. There is no dishonor in stumbling. In figure skating, a good thumping fall on the ice causes no real humiliation; what destroys one's dignity are the frantic writhings to *avoid* a fall. As a rower progresses in skill, crabs fall off in frequency, then become rare; proficiency extinguishes them. But as beginners we learn not to avoid crabs but rather to recover from them. We will catch crabs, but the boat stops only if they also catch us.

On the night before my first regatta, unable to sleep, I fretted about the next day's race, and crabs loomed large in my imagination. Six weeks earlier I had begun learning to row in eight-oared shells, and our club had entered a novice eight in a Charles River regatta called the Cromwell Cup. Having never raced in a boat before, I had no idea what to expect. But I knew enough to invent several dire scenarios about what might happen, and I was nervous.

As a beginning rower I had already caught many crabs in workouts, but in a race the stakes are far higher. A big crab severely disrupts the crew and may even cause the cox to stop the boat so that the afflicted rower can retrieve the oar and the crew reorganize itself. Such a pit stop generally puts the crew out of contention. Might I sabotage our chances by such a fatal mistake? — that dreadful threat had banished all but a couple hours of sleep. Yes, I wanted to row as well as possible, but what I prayed for was a crabfree race. Chances for this seemed good. The Cromwell Cup course is short, only 1,000 meters, which a good eight can cover in less than three minutes. We were *not* a good eight, but the crab season would be, at least, a short one.

I had begun my course in crustacean studies at age thirty-seven when, after years of watching the boats, I decided to get inside them again. My chance came when a few of Boston's coaches and elite rowers launched a new rowing club that would welcome all members of the community, and so was named Community Rowing. This club had a mission. Rowing has remained a small sport largely because few people have access to boats and water. Even in a major rowing center like Boston, where the Charles River winds through the heart of the city, the boathouses along its banks belong to colleges and private boat clubs, both of which screen their membership intensively. But Community Rowing opened its doors to anyone who was willing to pay its low fees ($25 per month in 1985) and wanted to learn to row. I qualified on both counts.

I was looking for a way back onto the water. Aside from my brief stint as a coxswain during college, my athletic activities had been confined to spectatorship and Frisbee. I hadn't considered rowing for Harvard's lightweight crew, mostly because I still felt that I could never qualify for a "real" sports team. But in my early twenties, as a graduate student, I gradually awoke to the fact that something was missing. A central source of my happiness — playing sports — had disappeared. I decided to take up squash again, found several partners, and played regularly. An intense hour on the squash court revived my childhood pleasure in my body; after a game, the exhaustion under a hot shower was delectable.

Then, in the mid-1970s, I lived in San Francisco for two years. There, amid a stream of sunny days, a supremely graceful tennis pro named Ben Chu taught me the game of tennis. When I returned to Boston I continued my two racquet sports and, with millions of others, joined the running boom. I began logging mileage around the Fresh Pond Reservoir in Cambridge and various other reservoirs and lakes, which seem to draw runners to them by a form of hydromagnetism. Our bodies are made mostly of water, and the deep attraction of lakes, rivers, and oceans may be a kind of homing instinct.

As the 1980s began, again in lockstep with millions, I joined a health and fitness club. There I could play tennis and squash year-round on indoor courts, swim, and work out on a battery of exercise machines — most important, those for weight lifting. I played mostly for fun, then for the challenge of mastery, and finally for fitness. There was also competition: I occasionally ran 5- or 10-kilometer foot races and played in tennis tournaments. A couple of tennis coaches helped my game, and though I won no trophies, I became an above-average club tennis player.

Thus at thirty-seven, reasonably fit and having achieved some degree of athletic prowess, I decided to try a team sport again. The romance of rowing continued to attract me. Each October I strolled among a quarter-million spectators at the Head of the Charles Regatta, and for eight months of the year, the flotilla of shells making their varied, graceful trips on the river hypnotized me. I was ready to join the fleet.

In part, my route back to the river was a professional one. During the 1970s I had earned a doctorate in sociology and then worked for a few years in health-related research. But in 1984 I decided to pursue an old and cherished dream and so left my job as a director of research in preventive medicine to become a full-time freelance writer. I began to write and publish magazine articles and soon decided to research the topic of rowing, thinking I could write something about it. I was not sure what form this would take: perhaps I could do a book or a screenplay capturing the magic of the slim boats that had been in my blood for two decades.

Surprisingly, it was very easy to find and interview elite rowers, and I mean *elite* rowers. Early on I met Abby Peck, who had just returned from rowing in the United States women's four at the 1984 Los Angeles Olympics. Abby and I sat down over mugs of coffee one morning at a café in Harvard Square, and when I looked up, I realized we had been talking rowing for three hours. Furthermore, it seemed as if the conversation had just begun.

Abby made the strivings on the water seem all the more entrancing, almost heroic. She portrayed rowers as a special breed of people, sharing exceptionally high levels of self-discipline, confidence, and camaraderie. She said that rowing's intense demands made you confront your limitations, forging a thorough self-examination. Strong commitment and integrity were assumed: an elite rower had to rise at five o'clock each morning and make the time to train, often twice a day. Even the best athletes could not earn money by rowing, yet they trained just as hard as pro football or basketball players, who made millions. Something very powerful was driving them from the inside.

Abby also noted that being part of a crew makes the individual shine: in rowing you pull harder and longer than you ever could alone because everyone else in the boat is depending on you. Rowing thus conflates individual and group effort: the boat is only as good as its weakest link, and each rower *is* that link. So an oarswoman tries to be as strong as possible, both for herself and her teammates. Perhaps, I thought, individual and group success were compatible after all. To me, they had seemed like oil and water.

In many ways, my temperament is a solitary one. I am a first-born, and for many years was an only child — my sister was born six years after me, my brother when I was ten. In my youth I contentedly spent many hours alone — roaming through the woods, playing the piano, inventing games, reading by the hour. In adult life I maintain similar habits. By 1984, I had launched myself on a highly independent writing career, working from an office in my own home. I had a great deal of freedom, but my daily routine was quite isolated from the lives of other people. Abby's remark about team-work — *the crew makes the individual shine* — stayed with me: could it be that I was holding myself back by operating as a lone wolf? Perhaps only sheer snobbery supported my belief that being a "joiner," participating in groups, stunts one's growth.

To me, group activity was ineffective and limiting. Meetings were tedious. Nothing good ever came out of a committee. Crea-tivity, I thought, varied with the inverse square of the size of the group: with two people present, you'd get one-fourth as much done as you would working alone; with three, one-ninth as much, with four, one-sixteenth as much, and so on. You could guarantee that a meeting of a hundred people would accomplish nothing useful.

But now teamwork began to attract me, even as my fears about collective culture resurfaced: I worried that a group like a crew might devour my autonomy. The team might ask me to do things I didn't want to do, and no lone wolf willingly embraces such fetters. Yet a group might also take me farther than I could go as an isolated individual, reigning as king of my own island; island life is fabulous, but it limits how far we can travel. Though I feared joining up, it seemed that I might miss out on something impor-tant by *not* joining.

Furthermore, I was thirsty for community. I had grown up in a real community; it was part of my soul. But human connections of that type had long vanished from my experience. Although I have spent almost all my adult life in metropolitan Boston, I am not by nature an urban creature: my mother came from a Pennsylvania farm family, and my father grew up in the small New Jersey town of fifteen thousand where I was born. When I was four, we moved to a residential area surrounded by an unspoiled forest in a largely undeveloped township nearby.

The woods, my first and best playground, bordered our yard. I spent countless hours there climbing trees, building forts, kicking through leaves in autumn. In our enclave, I knew all the children and adults as well as my classmates at school. When I began high school we moved back to town, where every street, park, and store was familiar. My father, a much-beloved citizen, had begun his career as a messenger at one of the town's two banks, and over the years he rose to become its president and chairman of the board. My mother, a full-time mom, was equally cherished by her friends and very much a part of the community. My dad graduated from the high school in 1938, and twenty-seven years later I did the same; 250 other students graduated with me, and though I didn't know each one well, I knew who everyone was. To me, that is a working definition of a community.

Such a sense of belonging nourishes the soul. When I left home to attend college, I had the good fortune to find myself in another human-scale community. Harvard separated its upperclass students into nine houses — residential complexes of 350–450 students each. As a member of Leverett House, I ate, studied, played, and socialized mostly with my friends and classmates there. Once again, I knew who everyone was, and that felt like home.

But after college, when I entered graduate school and rented an apartment, life shifted into an urban mode. The homelike feeling vanished, and I missed it. I miss it still, and it seems that we all do: the loss of community is the central heartbreak of America in the late twentieth century. Where neighborhoods and personal ties once linked people, now, it seems, only electronic media unite us. And even television is splitting into a narrowcasting Babel.

Yet we can still taste community through shared passions — like sports. When I began learning to row, I had no idea I was joining a riverborne village, but the name Community Rowing turned out to be accurate. By joining a crew I not only became part of an eight-oared team but of a rowing club — and a river community, a floating tribe, a fellowship in boats.

Common experience knits us together. Rowers undergo certain initiation rites; we have all caught crabs, sucked wind, risen reluctantly before dawn, and struggled with balancing a finicky boat. This communal past forges a tacit understanding, a feeling of joint endeavor, a sense that we are aspiring to the same goals. In our post-industrial society, such shared histories may be our best approximation of village life.

The newcomer to the rowing tribe, like the immigrant entering most groups, begins at the bottom. Having endured the privations at the lowest rung of rowing society gives the floating village a common history: we all rose from the bottom. When I first started at Community Rowing, I went out with my fellow beginners in a barge: a hulking, two-ton raft with eight port oars along one side and eight starboards on the other. Between them ran a wooden walkway, which allowed our coach, Lisa Goodhue, to stroll between the port and starboard oar banks and give advice to each novice, adding her wisdom to the ongoing tutelage of trial and error. The barge is a rock-solid craft whose stability allowed us to concentrate on the fundamentals of the rowing stroke. Our barge lumbered slowly but relentlessly up the river, not without a certain majesty. At times, sitting on one of its thwarts, I felt reincarnated as an ancient galley slave and imagined Lisa wielding a leather whip, wearing sandals with criss-crossed thongs up her calf. *Rowing is a sport that the French reserved for their convicts,* I recalled, *and the Romans for their slaves.*

Up from slavery: having mastered the basics, we graduated to eight-oared red cedar Pocock shells, sturdy and weighing about 300 pounds, and began learning to set up the boat. Community Rowing rented two shells from Harvard and launched them from Weld Boathouse, across the river from Newell. On summer mornings at 6 A.M., sixteen novice rowers and two coxswains filled these Pococks and rowed our morning workout with Lisa following in her motor launch. Two more boats went out at 5:30 P.M. The afternoon rowers dubbed one shell the *Cocktail Hour* and lettered that name on her bow with black electrician's tape. The *Cocktail Hour* was christened with a dry martini.

To experienced rowers, an eight is a very stable platform, a boat so large and weighty, especially when loaded with a crew, that the rower can focus on applying power rather than setting up the shell. In our novice eight it was nothing like this. On every stroke the shell wobbled fearfully. As we fought its pitch and yaw, occasionally some sardonic oarsman might bellow a comment like, "Rock 'n' roll is here to stay!" But if we lacked skill, we at least had that deficit in common. Shared flaws bond us. Like many novice crews, we salved our inadequacies with camaraderie and, occasionally, humor: after a crab-bitten row, when someone asked how it had gone, I might dryly observe that there had been *a little crustacean action* out there.

Over weeks, then months, of five-days-a-week practices with my crewmates, I gradually learned to set up a shell. One does this by feel, playing by the inner ear. We sense the shell going down to port and compensate for the list, adjusting the height of our oar handles to level the boat. But one must not surrender fully to pliancy; as in other intimate relations, while responding to each other, we need to maintain our own center of gravity. While reacting to imbalances, I keep my own weight and body position — legs, pelvis, torso, shoulders, arms, head — centered over the imaginary keel. With our personal balance intact, we can address the shared condition.

In the Cromwell Cup, our crew is racing in an eight, which is a sweep boat, as opposed to a sculling boat. The oars themselves are also called sweeps and sculls. A sweep — at about 12½ feet — is longer, with a wider shaft and blade than a scull, which measures about 9½ feet. Rowing sweeps, you hold one oar in both hands, whereas a sculler controls two oars, one in each hand. (In a single you must scull, since a lone sweep rower, pulling on only the port or starboard side, would travel eternally in circles, like a penitent in Dante's *Inferno,* condemned for one-sidedness.)

Sweep rowers specialize: they are either ports or starboards. This is like being left- or right-handed, except that sweep preferences do not correspond to throwing, writing, or doing anything else with a favored hand. Furthermore, unlike lefties, ports are about as numerous as starboards in the population.

Eight-oared shells number their seats from the bow: the seat nearest the bow is #1 (called "bow"), the next is #2, and so on up to the #8 seat, the sternmost rowing position. The #8 seat is the stroke seat, and its occupant, also called the stroke, sets the rowing cadence — which, ideally, the rest of the crew sedulously follows. There are variations, but the classic way to rig an eight-oared boat has even-numbered seats — stroke, #6, #4, and #2 — rowing the port oars, while the odd-numbered ones — #7, #5, #3, and bow — row starboard. At #3, I was a starboard, near the middle of the boat though not at its very heart.

The different seats in a racing shell, like different positions on a soccer or baseball team, favor athletes with certain talents. Since the stroke sets the cadence, steadiness and reliability are paramount; a good stroke rows to an internal metronome, ticking off a consistent rhythm. Strokes can sense subtle shifts in tempo and often have aggressive, competitive personalities because they lead the crew in a very concrete sense during a race. One coach once jokingly claimed that the key qualities of a good stroke were a strong jaw and red hair — because "the jaw is the seat of the will" and red hair signifies a fiery temperament.

The other half of the stern pair, the #7 oar, is the "starboard stroke" — since all the starboard rowers follow the #7 oar's cadence — and needs similar gifts for the same reasons. Coaches typically put their most powerful athletes in the #6, #5, #4, and #3 seats — the "engine room" in the middle of the boat. This is the place for behemoths who can apply raw, primal force, really bending the oars, although sound technique is essential here, as elsewhere. The engine room of a men's intercollegiate crew will typically include oarsmen who are over 6 feet tall and who weigh between 185 and 220 pounds. Not bulky like football linemen, they have long, strong bodies. Long legs, especially long thigh bones, lengthen the stroke and increase leverage on the oar.

The bow pair — bow and #2 — are usually two of the smaller, quicker athletes. They are often technically polished rowers, notable for their finesse. Sitting up near the bow magnifies their impact on how the shell steers, so they must be precise. Some coaches want the bow pair to be a bit quicker than the other crew members so they can stay with the stroke while sitting such a distance away.

The #3 oar is the bridge between the bow pair and the engine room, in the transitional zone between power and finesse; desirably, #3 can apply both qualities to the oar. The #3 seat may be the least specialized one, a place for a good all-arounder. After a particularly good workout or race, we who have rowed at #3 sometimes decide that this is the seat calling for the most complete athlete. On the other hand, some coaches fill the #3 seat with their least proficient athlete — *Could that be me?* — the rower who fits in nowhere else. Perhaps my first race at #3 would give me a clue to whether I was the crew's Renaissance man or its pariah.

Over my six years of rowing sweeps, I sat in every seat at one time or another. I am naturally a starboard but can also row port; on one memorable day the coach asked me to row port, then told me I'd be stroking the boat, then announced that we would be racing scrimmage pieces that day. (Yes, I survived — barely. Somehow we even won most of the pieces.) Our Community Rowing boats did not train like a college crew, in which a rower usually sits in the same seat every day. Unless we were preparing for a big regatta like the Head of the Charles, our club eights might change lineups daily, since the available roster varied with every workout.

Each seat in the boat offers unique sights, sounds, and feelings. The bow seat, for example, is the chilliest position, especially when rowing into a headwind, since it acts as a windbreak for the rest of the crew. Rowing in the engine room places one at the center of a line of moving bodies and may enhance the feeling of being enmeshed with the gears of effort. Here, the prodigious expenditure of kilocalories inspires a certain abandon, no doubt augmenting one's own muscular output.

The stroke seat offers both anguish and glory. Stroking a ragged crew can be an ordeal. Suppose, for example, that the rowers behind you are rushing up their slides as they approach the catch. This means that about half a ton of humanity is throwing their momentum at your back as you attempt to begin each stroke and move the boat in the very direction they are coming from. It feels like wading cautiously into heavy surf, treading delicately over seashells — then being hit with a strong undertow. Poor crews unconsciously sabotage the stroke's efforts. When momentum runs counter to the leader — whether stroking an eight or governing a country — that leader becomes the target, sitting in the seat of vulnerability. But when things go well, stroking a smooth-running eight enlarges our sense of ourselves: it octuples our every action. With this multiplier effect working for us, we feel like a force of nature.

In that case, only another natural force can oppose us. And so we race. Today, at the starting line, our Community Rowing eight is about to find its place in the natural order. Four novice crews are in this race; none of us has ever competed in an organized regatta. (That officially defines a novice event.) Now we are about to launch from the dock and row to the starting line. We complete our preparations: tying the shoelaces that hold our feet into the foot stretchers, checking that the gate atop the oarlock is secure and that the seat rolls easily in its tracks. Corinne, our coxswain, orders: "Count down from bow when ready!" This commands each of us, once we have assured ourselves that we are indeed ready to race, to call out our seat number. The roll call is a public commitment, a declaration that you are not just "ready to go" but ready to *go*. Tone of voice can even convey strength of intention: "*Six!*"

The countdown starts: "Bow!" "Two!" Then my turn: "Three!" After Jeff, the #4 man, counts off, there is a pause; Daniel at #5 is making sure that the wing nuts on his foot stretchers are tightly screwed down; it will not do to have them work loose during the race. The foot stretchers are the angled platforms that we push against to drive the legs down, pushing the sliding seat backward and so pulling the oarblade through the water. They are the ground on which we stand; their stability is the launching pad for our motion. Finally, Daniel is satisfied. The countdown finishes and we shove off from the dock.

When he invaded a foreign country, Julius Caesar burned his ships so that his soldiers would feel they must conquer the country or die; retreat would be impossible. Once we have launched, we are in the reverse situation: we have our boat, but we cannot return to land until we have conquered, or have been vanquished.

A solid rubber ball, called a bow ball, protects the tip of a racing shell's bow. Bow balls prevent damage when, inevitably, shells "kiss" — or slam into — things like docks and other boats. More important, they prevent rowers from being impaled on the sharp tip of a shell in case of a boat crash. Ideally, a race begins with all the bow balls in perfect alignment, the spheres equidistant from the finish line, like some rare astrological conjunction. This is crucial because the first bow ball across the finish line wins, and the second one is sometimes only hundredths of a second behind. Yet achieving this fair alignment poses maddening problems because the competitors are afloat; instead of staying put, they drift. Getting several shells ready to start can take a vexingly long time. Inside the boats, our prolonged state of readiness becomes a form of torture.

Bigger regattas often use stake boats, rowboats that originally were tethered to stakes sunken into the riverbed or lake bottom. Nowadays, anchors usually hold the stake boats fast. A volunteer in each one grips the racing shell's stern to stop it from floating forward. But the coxswain still must cope with the river current and lateral drift; having found a steering point, the cox stays on it through slight adjustments, generally by asking one of the two rowers nearest the bow to take a stroke or two.

It is quiet before the race; once the crew has warmed up, the cox minimizes talk on the way to the starting line and while waiting there. The silence allows a gathering of energies, and perhaps induces a state conducive to creation.

Starting anything demands outsize investments of energy. To change rest into motion, nothing into something, requires a concentrated initial input. Whether it be tulip bulbs, start-up capital, or pregnancy, occasions of birth demand rich infusions of energy — nutrients, money, love. Infancy, a stage of rapid growth, is hungry for resources. Often, beginnings mean new physical structures — like flower stalks, factories, or human bodies — that demand abundant raw materials. Starting can also mean setting a new course or simply accelerating, both of which also require disproportionately strong doses of energy.

In a regatta, the stage of rapid growth is the racing start —
several short, quick strokes that get the boat moving. A 60-foot
300-pound shell loaded with nearly a ton of athletes' bodies has
tremendous inertia; the first few strokes rouse this leviathan to
racing speed. We will row our first stroke at "three-quarters slide"
(using only three-quarters of the length of the tracks along which
our seats slide), take the second stroke at half-slide, the third at
three-quarters, then lengthen out to full slide on the fourth stroke.
These shortened strokes are like first and second gears in a car:
they get the vehicle up to cruising speed.

Our coxswain raises one hand above her head to signal the
starter that we are not yet ready to go, but once our shell is pointed,
she lowers it to her side and grips the rudder. The other coxswains'
hands are also down. Our muscles bunch up, nerves keen with
tension. Poised at the catch, three-quarters of the way up our
slides, all eight blades squared and buried in the water, we ache to
push off against the foot stretchers. We have become that drawn
arrow, ready to fly to the finish line on the starter's release.

The starter raises his megaphone and explains the sequence he
will use. Then, in a measured cadence, excitement spilling from his
voice — *this is real* — calls out the starting commands: "*Are* you
ready? *Ready* all! *ROW!*"

We explode against the foot stretchers; legs drive the pelvis back
and we push our shell out into the course, into life. "*Three*-quar-
ters! *Half*-slide! *Three*-quarters! *FULL* slide!" shouts our cox, the
aria of a racing start. The pitch of the engines of the officials' and
coaches' boats whines upward as they begin following the race:
we all power up together. Our strokes lengthen out and we take
"twenty high," a score of strokes at a high rating (for our novice
crew, "high" means 32 strokes per minute), accelerating to race
velocity. We could not last at 32 for the entire race; our crew would
"fly and die," burning out and folding toward the end. We aren't

physically fit enough to row that high for that long. But, luckily, the human body keeps a small cache of anaerobic energy in reserve, a shot of power for short-term efforts. For our racing start, we spend this biological start-up capital; yes, we *can* row twenty strokes at 32.

Under way now, we row in our ragged novice way, yet the shell actually cruises along fairly well. After our twenty high we bring our rate down to 26 — a transition called the settle — where we will row the body of the race. I concentrate on the lower back of Jeff, the #4 oarsman, aiming to synchronize myself with his motions and hence the rest of the crew's, and also monitor the oar-blade of Denny at #7, the starboard stroke. Throwing myself into the effort, I try to keep the boat set, driving my blade through the water as our coach has taught me to do, pulling as hard as I can. The shouts of all four coxswains mix in counterpoint as oars bite the water and the shells surge ahead. On every stroke, the steersmen's tumult is punctuated by the thunderous rhythmic *thump* of eight oar shafts pounding against oarlocks as they dig into the river — a noisy, wild spectacle teetering between anarchy and order, chaos with an objective. It's war out there. This is a naval engagement, excitement mingling with fear and the possibility of glory. The brain tells the bloodstream: *this is life or death.*

Then fears become disasters. In midrace, our shell tilts treacherously to starboard, digging the starboard oars deep into the water. Three of us manage to extract our oars cleanly. But I do not. My blade stays submerged a half-second longer than everyone else's, slamming the oar handle into my rib cage, roughly shoving me and my seat backward. It's a nasty little crab, the nemesis I had prayed to avoid. Hands pinned against my chest, I push the handle down hard and pop the blade out of the water. Somehow I keep my seat moving and don't break the crew's rhythm. Shaken, I rejoin the cadence but the crab has rattled me; I've dodged a bullet but now worry that another one might be coming.

Such broodings are worse than useless; they divert attention from the task at hand and so become self-fulfilling prophecies: ten strokes later I make a classic beginner's goof, feathering my blade underwater. Feathering means turning the blade's face upward during the recovery phase of the stroke (when the oars are above the water) to minimize air resistance and clear the water easily. But my premature, submerged feather amounts to trying to pry a bladeful of water out of the river. This will not work: the river jealously guards its vital fluids and holds them fast. My oar gets stuck again, then bursts out of the water at an oblique angle. This time the crab yanks the oar handle away from me; it propels itself forward and thumps Jeff's back. Still moving with the crew, I reach out and recapture it, then resume rowing — like running alongside a merry-go-round, then jumping on at the proper moment.

This race is becoming a fiasco. But things settle down and I start rowing effectively again. I have almost put these disasters out of my mind when a third crab hits. I think, *Why me?* then quickly reach the unhappy conclusion that the cause is not some Neptunian demon, but the #3 oarsman. This time I have simply pulled in too high, digging my blade into the depths, where it remains; I am forced into an extreme layback position at the end of the stroke, as if on a chaise longue. I would be reclining into the lap of the #2 man, Peter, if he were not also finishing his stroke, hence tilted backward himself. With a mighty shove I push the handle down along my chest and free the oar from the aquatic vise. We continue bulling ahead.

With 300 meters to go our boat is dead last — *surely because of those crabs* — yet somehow we are not far behind the other three boats. Then our crew finds its rhythm. We move up on the competition, which, admittedly, is less than stiff. With 200 meters left our cox calls a sprint, and we again take the rate up to 32 while staying together. There is another reserve tank of anaerobic fuel, which we tap for the final strokes. We power past the other three boats to win the race.

It takes a moment or two before word of our victory reaches us. To me, this seems miraculous (*Was there some mistake?*), knowing that I caught three — count them, *three* — crabs during the race. Our finishing sprint must have saved the day.

Moments later our crew stands on the dock of the Riverside Boat Club as winners of the novice eight event at the 1985 Cromwell Cup Regatta. I feel a surge of winner's joy; at this moment all is right with the world, not just here, but everywhere. The afterglow lights the rest of the day, and during the following week I will often recall this winning moment with pleasure.

On the dock, I confess my amazement at our win to Joe, our #6 man, explaining that I personally had registered three crabs in the race. "When was that?" he asks, incredulous. "I didn't know anyone had caught a crab — I never felt a thing." Absolution now joins the euphoria of winning my first crew race: sitting only three seats ahead of me, Joe had felt *nothing*. He shakes his head and asks, "How in the world did you get those crabs back so fast?"

I muse on that for a moment and then give him the truest answer I can summon: "Lots of experience."

Lots of experience. Theorizing on the subject will not teach us to handle crabs. There is a parallel to this in the practice of law. Naturally, every legal client wants an attorney with good judgment. But how does a lawyer develop good judgment? The paradoxical answer: lots of experience with bad judgment.

In reality, lots of bad judgment can simply be a series of attempts to find one's way. It is impossible to choose a career, for example, by using your head to figure out what you want to do. It is not an intellectual process.

In my own case, while I earned a doctorate in sociology, even as a graduate student I knew an academic career was not for me. The professor's life was too cerebral for my temperament, and I lacked the enthusiasm for scholarship that would be required to excel in academia.

Yet social science research opened some doors to what academics call the real world. I wrote my doctoral dissertation on television entertainment production in Hollywood, where I spent a summer at Norman Lear's company, which then had nine sitcoms on the air. At the Haight-Ashbury Free Medical Clinics in San Francisco, I worked on drug abuse research, and in Boston, interviewed drug addicts for a study of heroin addiction. Later I became director of research for the state's division of preventive medicine and even published scientific articles in the *New England Journal of Medicine.*

Yet I had no real passion for this work. Research was reasonably satisfying, but I wanted a career that was unreasonably satisfying. And so at thirty-six, I became a writer. For the next five years, most of my small income came from freelance magazine work, but I also tried dozens of other professional and semiprofessional pursuits. A speaker's agency in New York booked me on the college lecture circuit, where I gave a multimedia show satirizing masculine images in advertising. I learned video editing, worked at a cable television station, and made my own music videos. I wrote a screenplay, several film treatments, and a few proposals for book-length nonfiction — all of which I attempted, with little success, to market.

The Audi automobile company retained me as a field producer to interview and videotape Audi drivers for a promotional film. I performed stand-up comedy, learned to play the alto saxophone, wrote advertising copy and promotional literature, studied acting, produced a short film on indoor rowing machines, and wrote market research reports on focus groups. Several darkroom courses prepared me to try fashion photography, so, using friends as models, I shot a portfolio of glamour shots and portraits. I wrote a children's Christmas story from the point of view of a piece of pie that was about to be eaten.

Many of us have such diverse backgrounds: our life work reveals itself through trial and error. Each experience teaches us about our aptitudes and our preferences as well as showing us where we lack desire or talent. Tacking along a career path, every false start is important. The zigzagging actually never stops; we never "arrive" but continually refine how our work expresses who we are. Even after many years in a field, we may find ourselves on some surprising new tacks.

The essential point is that we cannot work it through theoretically. Enjoyable work satisfies the emotions, the social instincts, the body, and the spirit as well as the intellect. To find our calling, we must listen to all of these inner voices, which speak from, and to, the soul.

The more mistakes we commit, the faster our learning curve slopes skyward. Actually, it is not mistakes but *attempts* that are the oxygen of success. Most real learning comes from trial and error; therefore the essential thing is a plethora of trials — a profligate, heedless, excessive abundance of trials. *The road of excess,* wrote William Blake, *leads to the palace of wisdom.*

Mistakes are not failures; they are results that diverge from our expectations. We act while holding a mental image of the consequences. Call this image an intention. But reality thumbs its nose at our intention: the result isn't what we imagined. This is a mistake, a trial that became an error. Such moments open us up to the world. Errors admit fresh air. They guide us through a door of perception, offering escape from the solipsism of our minds. Mistakes shine a spotlight on our model of reality and show us its flaws. Unexpected outcomes help us refine our picture of nature.

After making an error, the essential thing is to notice what happened. Precisely how did reality differ from our image? That gap holds new information. Errors ought to fascinate us. But to receive their message, we must be concentrating on our task, rather than ourselves. Nature withholds her lessons from those who gaze only inward. A mistake informs us about our endeavor, not ourselves; it illuminates a new aspect of what we must do to succeed. Failures are road signs — NOT THIS WAY — marking the route to success.

In dealing with errors, a crucial variable is *recovery time*. A short recovery time between a "failure" and the next attempt embodies the character trait that we call resilience. Nothing accelerates progress more than resilience.

Imagine being a young actor going on auditions. Like composing music or writing poetry, acting heaps rejection onto every aspirant, even the gifted. Suppose you show up for an audition and 120 other talented young actors are also reading for the part. Not surprisingly, you do not get the role.

You doubt your ability to succeed in this merciless profession, as anyone must, and rejection only feeds your doubts. Now the real question: after being turned down, do you go home, take to your bed, and languish in discouragement? Do you spend six months wondering about your abilities before going on another audition? To do so is to implement a long recovery time. Long recovery times lengthen the feedback cycles between trials and so postpone learning.

Consider another path. After being turned down, you feel the discouragement of rejection and sense yourself sliding into self-pity — but then you notice what is happening and *immediately kill that inner dialogue.* Interpreting rejection this way has you going out on another audition tomorrow. Short recovery times produce fast feedback cycles; they accelerate learning. We shorten our recovery times by understanding how to deal with errors. In a nut-shell: *don't take them personally*. Mistakes are our mentors; they are, in a sense, feedback from the gods.

For many years I have studied and played classical, blues, and jazz piano. Late one afternoon I was trying to master the Aria from Bach's *Goldberg Variations*. This is not one of the more difficult pieces in the piano repertoire, but nonetheless it challenged the keyboard skill I then possessed. One particular passage was defeating me. Everything went fine until the seventh bar, where I continued to replicate the same error. I kept starting over and trying again, hoping that sheer momentum would somehow blast me through the difficult passage. It was doing no such thing.

Finally I decided to stop butting my head against a wall. I would focus solely on the one recalcitrant measure. But I merely proceeded to repeat my previous strategy in miniature — playing the bar over and over, wrongly every time, and wrong in exactly the same way each time. All I was doing was hearing my mistake more often.

This became terrifically frustrating. I was getting enraged at this stubborn bar of music. *Why is this so hard? It doesn't look like anything special on the score.* The diabolical J. S. Bach had apparently booby-trapped this innocuous-looking piano piece with a passage that required virtuoso abilities. I began questioning my talent as a pianist and even my capacity to learn — not just music, but anything.

After ten minutes of struggle, I admitted that I was not going to bull my way through this passage by repetition. I took a deep breath, sat back on the piano bench, and examined the score carefully. When I put my hands back on the keyboard I drastically slowed the tempo, and in slow motion, I finally noticed what was happening. First, I saw the precise place where my error began: I was striking the key just below the correct note. Another slow-motion rehearsal revealed that I was fingering the preceding note with my middle, rather than index, finger. This variant fingering created an awkward transition to the following note, and hence my error. Once I corrected the fingering, suddenly the passage played flawlessly. A few more renditions to lock in the proper sequence, and I was back into the flow of the Aria.

Repetition is not enough: practice alone does not make perfect. I could have spent another hour repeating that passage without getting anywhere. What made a difference was shifting the quality of my attention to the task. First, I stopped wallowing in frustration and second-guessing myself. Then, by slowing down, I started to notice what I was actually doing; instead of spinning my wheels, mired in the repeating patterns of my mind, I switched to an external focus. This opened a window to sunlight that illumined a path to success.

In a single scull, one very effective mode of training is simply to *feel the boat*. Ideally our attention should focus on the boat and not our own bodies. Our bodily sensations are useful insofar as they tell us about the state of the boat. Listen to the shell, feel your boat, respond to its needs. The boat wants to go fast, is designed to go fast, so our ultimate task is to attend to the boat and serve its desires. Getting our attention off ourselves and onto our shell is, in a sense, the only training program we need. Feeling the effect of each stroke on the shell opens up a constant, rich stream of feedback that will teach us how to row this boat to its maximum potential. The shell is the ultimate coach.

As I rowed in sweep boats over the years, accumulating thousands of miles on the water, the quantity and quality of my experience began to make me an oarsman. I also learned about the sport through my work as a journalist. In the mid-1980s I began to publish articles on rowing. I wrote several cover stories for the U.S. Rowing Association's magazine, *American Rowing*, and contributed pieces to *Harvard Magazine* and *Sports Illustrated*. In 1987 *Town & Country* assigned me to write a feature article on the Henley Royal Regatta in England, an opulent five-day event that is the sport's oldest and most famous race. After Henley, I flew to Switzerland for another big regatta at Lucerne, then traveled in a van, pulling a rack truck loaded with racing shells, with coaches from the Italian national team to Piediluco, Italy, a tiny lake village in the Umbrian hills.

In this remote spot, unchanged in many ways since the Renaissance, the Italian rowing team had its training facility. Their Norwegian coach, Thor Nilssen, had headed Italy's program for several years after notable successes with crews from Norway, Sweden, and Spain. Thor is a very bright man whose organizational and coaching methods have changed the sport, and he has an excellent sense of humor. For example, one day in July, he and I stood together for a few minutes on the dock at Piediluco, watching two Italian eights row. I was seeing two boats moving gracefully across a lovely lake on a summer afternoon. Thor was seeing the same thing as well as much else that was invisible to my uninitiated eyes. Finally, in his singsong Norwegian accent, he broke the silence. "You know, Craig, we could really have a good time around here," he said, "if it weren't for all this damned *rowing*."

Thor had developed advanced ways to measure a rower's power output using a device known as the ergometer. An erg is a unit of energy in physics (equal to the work done by a force of one dyne acting over a distance of one centimeter). Hence an ergometer is, literally, a device that measures energy output. But in the rowing world, ergometer is a synonym for rowing machine (colloquially called an erg). Sophisticated rowing machines — most crews use one called the Concept II ergometer — have electronic meters that can quite precisely indicate how much physical work a rower generates on each stroke. Ergometer tests are one method rowing coaches use to evaluate their athletes.

One day Thor and I mused together over a puzzling fact. Ergometer scores, he said, could help a coach understand the effects of training methods on the athletes' fitness levels. Other physiological tests could measure things like a rower's maximal oxygen-uptake capacity (VO_2 max) — quantifying the ability to burn oxygen, the fuel of endurance. Years of intense training can build these parameters to their full potential, but genetic endowment ultimately places a ceiling (Thor called it a *roof*) on how much they can increase. Nonetheless, many elite rowers had shown that even without changing any of these scores and without altering their basic rowing technique, over years of training they could still get better at moving boats. What could make them improve so?

Thor hypothesized that with experience, the rowers' *economy* improves: they can do the same work with less energy by becoming more efficient. When we perform an activity for the first time, he said, it takes lots of concentration. But after 10,000 repetitions, we can do it with less physical and mental energy. And after 100,000 times there is even more economy.

Without conscious intent, these elite oarsmen that Thor coached, like all top rowers, had streamlined their strokes, eliminating pointless thoughts and needless motions. Experience eroded any actions that did not enhance boat speed. In this regard rowing resembles writing: recall the classic advice that William Strunk, Jr., gave in *The Elements of Style* (1918): "Vigorous writing is concise. A sentence should contain no unnecessary words, a paragraph no unnecessary sentences, for the same reason that a drawing should have no unnecessary lines and a machine no unnecessary parts." Like a sentence, a rowing stroke — in fact, any gesture — should omit needless motions.

Great athletes in all sports exhibit such economies. In the last 200 meters of a crew race or the fifth set of a tennis match, they can outlast opponents, in part because all along they have used fewer muscles and consequently less energy to get there. While beginners deploy many muscle groups to pull an oar or swing a tennis racquet, elite athletes use only those muscles that are needed. This simplifies form. Efficiency brings fluidity and grace. My tennis mentor, Ben Chu, floated like a t'ai chi master at the baseline; it seemed that he barely moved a step or two in either direction, hardly exerting himself during a lesson. Yet he would return every ball sprayed across the net by his panting, scrambling, lunging student.

In mathematics, an elegant proof of a theorem uses the fewest possible steps, taking the most direct route to its result. There are lengthier, less imaginative pathways, but mathematicians dismiss these as "brute forcing" the problem. Beginners may need brute force, but the cognoscenti seek elegance, which embodies beauty. On this point science and art agree.

Good form in sports is almost always beautiful. Fluidity and ease flow from the same spring as does power. In athletics, with few exceptions, if it *looks* good, it *is* good.

Grace has no upper limit. While the improvements due to increased physical capacity are finite — they have a *roof* — we do not know where gains due to economy of motion end. The limiting factors seem to be age and motivation. Most athletes never reach their personal horizon: they stop before having exhausted their potential, usually because their motivation to improve declines. As rowers age, other priorities — families and careers, for example — grow in importance, and the sport no longer commands the same centrality it did when they were in their mid-twenties.

Leading a more balanced life exacts a price in athletic attainment; although a sport may remain important, maturation broadens the range of our involvements. Such diffusion of energies can surely support a healthier, more satisfying life. Exceptionally high achievers, however, often put all their eggs in the basket called work. This can lead to excellence and fame, but it has its costs. Picasso, Mozart, and Gandhi were no paragons in their personal lives; they attained ambitions for themselves and for posterity, but paid — and exacted — a high price in human relationships.

As I became part of the rowing tribe, I gradually recaptured that sense of belonging that infuses a community. Perhaps I did not know who everyone on the river was, but I did know many of them, and they knew me; we hailed each other in passing on the water and frequently showed up at the same social events. In time, the rowing tribe began to provide me with a kind of education in relationships, as music has also done.

Like the rowing of boats, playing music involves various social molecules. For example, the solo singer or instrumentalist shows us the possibilities of the individual acting alone. Duets mimic the close rapport, the give-and-take, of a couple or a pair of good friends. A jazz combo or a chamber music group like a string quartet illustrates the dynamics of a family. And a symphony orchestra, with its sections of strings, brass, woodwinds, and percussion instruments, offers a model of society functioning at its best — the varied soloists and sections cooperating to express harmony and counterpoint amid immense variety and contrast.

On the water, the single sculler is the soloist; pairs and doubles row as duets; fours and quads are the family units. An eight might resemble an extended family, or a large one. Rowing has no orchestra, although a boathouse, with its varied crews — freshman, junior varsity, varsity, third boats, fourth boats, all of these in lightweight and heavyweight versions — might be rowing's equivalent of a symphony. More than a hundred college oarsmen, for example, train in Harvard's Newell Boathouse in the course of a typical year, and they do form a society of sorts.

Certain irreducible dilemmas arise when human beings work together. The great advantage that a crew or string quartet has over a multicultural society is that the rowers or musicians share a fundamental agreement about collective purpose. Within that agreement, much remains to negotiate, but the common goal helps each member of the group to set aside personal agendas (also called ego) that conflict with the communal objective. Agreement on a destination gives the group cohesion.

Diversity can strengthen a team, but diversity per se is not necessarily helpful. What we seek on a team is a variety of attributes that contribute to the joint endeavor. For example, adding an overweight, out-of-shape athlete to a crew would surely add diversity of a sort, but not the sort that enhances boat speed. Similarly, a tone-deaf musician is unlikely to help a symphony orchestra. Strong teams balance variety with unity around a clear sense of purpose.

Social lessons also emerge from the physical world. In the boats, catching a crab penalizes the rower for nonconformity. While idiosyncratic behavior has its place, that place is not on a crew. In a team boat, individualism is a disruption, a form of antisocial deviance that undermines the common effort. For the boat to move its fastest, rowers must synchronize their strokes as perfectly as possible. Many different rowing styles have produced fast crews; whatever the technique, the crucial factor may be simply getting eight people to do the same thing together.

Crews have little use for "stars." Single sculls are different: rowing alone, we report to no one, so stardom is not only allowed but encouraged. Some single scullers have become world champions while rowing in highly unorthodox ways. However, as soon as another rower sits with us in the boat, relationship becomes a factor; working in concert becomes critically important. In a pair (two sweep rowers) or a double (two scullers) we must row *with* our partner, else the boat moves slowly and choppily. Pairs are especially sensitive. With only one port and one starboard oar to balance the craft, a failure of symmetry can capsize the shell. Fours (four sweep rowers) and quads (four scullers) further submerge the ego. In an eight, coordination is paramount, since even the most powerful rower is still only one-eighth of the lineup. The crew is only as strong as its weakest link, and each rower is that link. Some claim that rowing an eight is just about the most sociable thing there is.

Excellence in a crew thus resembles excellence in beagle dogs. Beagles are a fungible breed, known for their genetic uniformity. In fact, certain kinds of research on canine brains use only beagles because they are so reliably identical. As with brains, so with bodies: genetically, they tend to be interchangeable.

Historically, this has been a disadvantage at dog shows, where the judges look for superlative specimens. The blue ribbon for each breed (Best of Breed) goes to the dog epitomizing the best traits of its particular breed, and one of these exemplars eventually wins the Best of Show award. Beagle fanciers sometimes complain that beagles rarely win Best of Show. They fail to grasp the implications of the breed's consistency. Most dog breeds vary widely in genetic makeup and so include outstanding individual specimens. But a beagle who varies from the norm is a mutant. In beagles, an outstanding specimen is defective: the *best* beagle is not a *good* beagle.

Similarly, a *star* rower is not a *good* rower. While there are a few athletes of such exceptional power and talent that they will add speed to any boat, for the most part, rowing well in crews means replicating the actions of others. The finely tuned rapport approaches a sexual blending of wills. The social discipline of rowing rewards coordination; crews exalt community over individuality.

In this respect rowing differs from most spectator sports, which sell stardom. The star performance — the home run, the slam dunk, the long touchdown pass — is the centerpiece of professional athletics. A basketball star like Michael Jordan towers above the multitude, not only for his skills, but for the entertainment value of his acrobatics; it is not just that he scores so many points, but *how* he scores them. As spectator sports merge with the entertainment industry, where audience appeal trumps all, this emphasis on spectacle is inevitable. However, it is a commercial priority, not an athletic one. In sports like rowing, which command no audience to speak of, showmanship is irrelevant. On the water, only performance matters.

Rowing is the oldest intercollegiate sport and may also be the one that has changed the least since Oxford and Cambridge first raced each other at Henley in 1829. When rowing began, baseball, football, and basketball did not exist. In the late nineteenth century there was a period when regattas attracted huge crowds and heavy betting. Corruption set in, and in response, the rowing establishment enforced a strict code of amateurism. Since then, crew has been a sport of doers, not spectators — of athletes, not audiences. Today, a handful of athletes at the pinnacle of the sport — a few Olympic gold medalists — can actually earn sizable sums from sponsorships. But rowing has never become a profit center like football, basketball, or ice hockey. There are no television contracts and no professional rowing leagues. Even for those who perform at world-class levels, the trials on the water remain, for the vast majority, an amateur endeavor.

These amateurs, however, are in deadly earnest. College and elite rowers undertake training regimes of breathtaking rigor, practicing twelve months a year, virtually every day of the week. Rowing makes tremendous physical demands. It requires vast reserves of stamina and is one of the few endurance sports (cross-country skiing is another) that brings all the major muscle groups — legs, back, arms, and shoulders — into play. Yet the spring racing season may be only five races long, each race lasting five to six minutes — half an hour of competition. The ratio of effort to glory is astoundingly high.

Inner drives push us out onto the water. The sport demands much but gives back no athletic scholarships, lucrative pro careers, or fan adulation. With so few extrinsic rewards, the inner payoffs need to be profound. At some point the means becomes the end; we must learn to love training. In the final analysis, each stroke becomes its own reward.

The passion that so many rowers display for the sport may simply reflect natural selection: anyone who is less than avidly committed soon disappears from the river. More than a century ago, speaking at the Yale Commencement, Justice Oliver Wendell Holmes, Jr., contemplated the oarsman's character:

> Why should you row a boat race? Why endure long months of pain in preparation for a fierce half-hour that will leave you all but dead? Does anyone ask the question? Is there anyone who would not go through all its costs, and more, for the moment when anguish breaks into triumph — or even for the glory of having nobly lost? Is life less than a boat race? If a man will give all the blood in his body to win the one, will he not spend all the might of his soul to prevail in the other?

Team and individual sports cultivate two sides of the human soul: the involved citizen and the self-actualizing individual. There is a human conundrum: while each of us is unique, we all resemble one another in countless ways. Different cultures polish either the head or tail of this coin. A society that exalts community stresses connections and similarities; an individualistic culture like the United States sharpens the distinctions that separate us.

Because crew demands identical, closely coordinated actions, some call rowing the ultimate team sport, the athletic endeavor that most completely erases individual egos in favor of group success. Some fanatics even use this fact to argue for the moral superiority of rowing, and sophomoric bumper stickers like ATHLETES ROW — OTHERS PLAY GAMES appear on their cars.

Paradoxically, we reach this high state of communality through solitary effort. Rowing is not like soccer, where someone's perfect pass can set you up to score, nor like baseball, where three team-mates execute a *pas de trois* to cut down a runner at the plate. Rowers intimately coordinate their efforts, yet they do not interact. In the boat, I sit alone in my seat and cope alone with the challenges of oar and water; in this, my teammates can offer scant help.

Thus we row together in solitude. To balance the boat, on each stroke I feel the boat's set and respond with my starboard oar. Again: it is like walking a tightrope while holding a long balance pole. But in crew, the pole is sawed in half. A sculler holds both halves, one in each hand. In sweep boats we hold only the port or starboard half and so must work with our mates to stay balanced on the rope that is our boat. A crew converses through the shell, just as a team of tightrope walkers might have dialogue through the rope, its telephone line. On the water, the boat is our fiber-optic cable.

Although balancing the boat is a joint endeavor, each rower must take full responsibility for the set. We cannot directly change what our crewmates are doing, and we are all constantly making mistakes. (This is true of even the best rowers; their mistakes simply occur within a narrow range.) All we can do is put our own house in order: tend to our own oar and our own seat, keep our body weight centered, and make adjustments that balance the boat. We must act as if the boat's fate rests in our hands alone. If all eight of us adopt this myth, the eight fictions will add up to one salutary fact: the boat will set up level, the aggregate result of actions performed in solitude.

In this light, consider the human immune system, which maintains another kind of balance. Your immune system preserves bodily integrity by identifying foreign invaders — bacteria, viruses, toxins — and eliminating them. It spots intrusions by checking the cell surface of suspect entities to compare their genetic identities with the code of your DNA, the biological signature that is "you." In the bloodstream, whatever is "not you" is trespassing, so the immune system destroys it: it was probably up to no good. This is why the body rejects organ transplants: their genetic signature clashes with our own, so the immune system attacks the foreign tissue; the transplant is alien to this biological community. Any system that preserves singularity — for example, a national government — defends borders in this way. Only the identity cards are different.

Yet immunity is not static; it evolves and in fact could be said to learn. Each foreign incursion stimulates the body to create new antibodies, new weapons to neutralize chicken pox, colds, measles. Children have no large arsenal of antibodies, so they fall prey to all the familiar diseases of childhood. Vaccinations imitate certain invaders and provoke the production of appropriate antibodies to meet the real invader and forestall actual illness. Each challenge teaches the immune system how it needs to grow, developing its singularity based on the troubles it has seen. The bloodstream becomes a palimpsest that reflects the environments through which it has passed.

Something like this happens in a good crew. As rowers develop their skills to higher levels, their evolution as individual athletes lets them respond more precisely and flexibly to one another and to fluctuations in the set of the boat. A fine rower can keep the boat set up, or nearly so, even with unskilled crewmates. Accomplished rowers listen to both the boat and crew, then precisely answer the needs of the moment. In making their responses, they can summon a wide repertoire of adjustments.

Thus, high-level teamwork, even in something as synchronized as rowing, avoids homogeneity. Amid unpredictable conditions, homogeneous groups perform at lower levels overall. They do not contain a wide enough array of skills to handle fluctuating environments like rivers — or high-technology industries. Amid rapidly changing conditions, monolithic organizations flounder badly because they lack adaptability. Their narrow repertoire of talents does not allow them to address new problems quickly and sensitively; they face stimuli that greatly outnumber their available responses.

In any sport, winning teams are rarely monolithic; championship rosters include a mixture of skills that provide several ways of overcoming opponents. World Series winners, for example, usually blend speed and power. If they cannot beat you with quickness, then they will beat you with muscle. In rowing, fast crews combine endurance, power, and perhaps finesse. Their diversity — including diversity *within* each athlete — is their strength.

In 1986, when I had been rowing for only two seasons, my friend Tom Tiffany and I had our entry accepted by the Head of the Charles Regatta, in the Championship Doubles event. That we were actually going to be in the big race came as something of a surprise. We decided to get some advice from a master oarsman and met one morning with our friend Tiff Wood, having paddled our double to the Cambridge Boat Club dock. He glanced at our boat and told us that our first problem was that we were rowing "a real tub." He advised us to find a better double, and we resolved to do exactly that.

Then Tiff took me out for a short row, to observe my sculling technique and offer whatever advice occurred to him. Tiff rowed bow and I stroked, so that he could see what I was doing. Never before or since have I had a chance to row with an oarsman of such a high caliber, and the experience made a lasting impression.

While training with Tom, I had gotten used to our struggles with setting up the double — our tipping, tilting progress interrupted by brief stretches of balance when we could actually take a few effective strokes. I was thus unprepared for what happened when Tiff and I shoved off from the dock. From the very first stroke I was in a different world. Magically, the boat set up steady as a rock and stayed set. And with Tiff rowing behind me, the shell's speed — even for this minimal, light workout — quickly eclipsed my known benchmarks. I was the same flawed sculler I had been two minutes earlier, but rowing with Tiff, I suddenly became a highly competent oarsman. He was a classic example of the kind of teammate who makes the athletes around him better than they are.

When we returned to the dock, I grinned and told Tom how, after this row, I had finally realized how incredibly gifted I was as an oarsman: Tiff somehow had brought out my innate talent and speed. Of course, my Superman cape vanished as soon as I resumed rowing with lesser mortals. But what lingered was a sense of how a world-class oarsman affects the boat. Even in a "tub," even when paired with the questionable oarsmanship of someone like myself, Tiff made the double move gracefully, efficiently. For him, the surrounding limitations, the shortcomings of boat and partner, were simply *inputs*, factors computed into the equation of making this shell go. Tiff was so individuated and so adaptable that our boat was immune even to the vagaries of a sculler like me.

As a crew of two, Tiff Wood and I were a microcosmic example of how teams can stretch their members' horizons. At the highest levels of sport, the best athletes in the world train in groups. *The crew makes the individual shine.* There is leverage, for example, in the phenomenon of accountability.

Rowers have a phrase that nicely epitomizes this: "taking the alumni option." Imagine awakening one morning in the darkness at five o'clock, then getting dressed to row. You emerge from your front door and a cold, driving rain pelts your face. You say to yourself, *The hell with this,* and decide to take the alumni option: you go back inside, forget that day's workout, and return, quite cheerfully, to bed.

This is the alumni option because students lack this alternative: on a school or college crew we must come to practice regardless of the weather. We show up no matter how we feel about it: teammates are counting on us to be there. This is being accountable to others: we have given our word, and they will hold us to it. The decision to train is no longer an individual choice but a social one.

Social decisions were made for me as an oarsman with Community Rowing. I had to do certain things in order to row: show up punctually at Weld Boathouse at 6 A.M. (being late would hold up the entire crew), be there regardless of the weather, help carry the oars and boat out of the boathouse and store them carefully after our row, obey the coxswain's and coach's commands. While on the water, the most basic freedom I gave up was the choice, at any moment, to row or not to row. While my crew was in motion, I had only one option: to row along with them.

This may sound obvious, but it is actually an overpowering fact: *you cannot stop rowing.* It matters greatly because, quite often, stopping seems like just about the best idea in the world. It is not, of course, that one literally cannot stop, but short of physical collapse, such a choice would be difficult to explain to one's coach and crewmates. It would be as if a member of a surgical team decided to take a coffee break in the middle of an operation: it is simply not done.

Consider a workout in which the coach tells us to row a three-minute piece, full pressure, at 30 strokes per minute. *Sounds simple: 90 strokes and we are done.* But we have already been rowing for an hour, and we are tired. Two minutes into the three-minute piece, my muscles are screaming for respite, and it seems that I cannot quite gulp enough air to satisfy the pleadings of my lungs. Left to my own devices — perhaps rowing in a single with no coach — I might decide to stop, or take the rating down to 26, or go to three-quarters pressure. Or I might decide that this was really meant to be a *two*-minute piece. But in the eight, I am accountable to my crew and coach; I cannot stop, no matter what my mind says. There is no alumni option.

The impulse to tank the workout occurs at all levels of sport. It is so universal that it resembles human nature. For example, in the early 1970s an oarsman named Dave Fellows rowed for the Harvard varsity, where he acquired the nickname "Whiteman." The sobriquet referred to the venerable joke in which the Lone Ranger says, "Tonto, old buddy, it looks like we've had it — we're surrounded by Indians," to which Tonto replies, "What you mean *we*, white man?"

Fellows got this nickname after a late afternoon practice when the crew had worked hard, tired itself out, and was ready to call it a day. Instead, Harry Parker raised his megaphone and told the coxswains to turn the boats around, announcing that "we're going to row two more three-minute pieces." Hearing this, Fellows turned to Parker and hollered, "What you mean *we*, white man?" This became a legendary remark, and Dave was "Whiteman" for the rest of his Harvard career. Later, when Fellows rowed for the U.S. national team, the nickname went international: the French called him *homme blanc,* to the Germans he was *Weissmann,* and at the Pan Am Games in Puerto Rico, he was greeted as *hombre blanco.*

The moral of the story is that even world-class athletes often feel like packing it in. So they train in groups, where accountability keeps them going when, practicing alone, they would have called it quits. One's personal limit is not a fixed quantity, nor is it separate from the social context. Playing tennis against a superb opponent can raise one's game, and just as surely, training with athletes who are willing to go one bridge farther up the river can take us to a horizon we would not have reached alone.

Similarly, breathing an atmosphere of excellence can encourage us to follow through on projects and complete them. Adverse conditions might persuade us to slow down or quit an endeavor, but we would fall short of the standards set by our family, friends, co-workers, or teammates. And so we persevere. Transcending our personal weaknesses in this way widens our concept of self. The expansion of consciousness involves admitting a wider spectrum of powers into our reality, gradually aligning our personal spectrum with the social and, eventually, the cosmic one.

Decades of work in exercise physiology and nutrition have greatly advanced our understanding of how to train bodies. Discoveries in this area will continue, but the learning curve has gone asymptotic: further improvements are likely to be marginal. A world-class athlete who is training twice daily with a state-of-the-art conditioning program is unlikely to break through to new levels of fitness. In strength, endurance, and flexibility, the evolution of the human body caps our progress; our organisms, as currently constructed, simply cannot do very much more. And genetic evolution moves at a glacial pace over many generations.

In contrast, the human mind can evolve instantly: a single thought can shift our whole attitude. One decision can change the pattern of the rest of my life. Unlike the body, the mind has no upper limit on how fast it can evolve. The effect of the mind on sports performance is the frontier of coaching.

The mental aspects of training and performance pose problems of communication between coaches and athletes. A rower who is trying to win a seat on a college varsity or a national team wants to appear in the best possible light. Therefore the athlete tends to conceal problems — sometimes even injuries — from the coach, because "problems" might hurt the rower's chances of making the team or of participating to the fullest extent and at the highest levels. Athletes even avoid such topics among their peers, who might be their rivals for a place on the team.

If admitting physical problems is difficult, frankness regarding mental shortcomings is nearly impossible. It is one thing to tell the coach "I'm getting painful twinges in my lower back at the end of a long piece; is there some physical therapy that could help?" It is quite another to say "Coach, I'm having trouble pulling my hardest when I get tired near the end of a race. I've got an urge to ease off a bit, to give myself a break. Can you suggest anything to toughen me up mentally?" The former is merely a physical problem, but the latter looks like a character defect. And while most of the body's problems are temporary, we tend to see character flaws as permanent. *No, there's nothing I can suggest except to find another sport. Go sabotage somebody else's team.*

Yet these are merely our conventional prejudices: athletes *can* change mental and emotional habits as well as physical idiosyncrasies. Helping them to handle such mental quandaries might be the greatest contribution a coach could make to a well-trained crew. Yet such interventions will remain rare as long as the incentive structure penalizes athletes for confessing a problem. When the truth cannot be told, the underlying situation remains frozen in place, so the athlete's mental habit will persist, perhaps forever.

My years of rowing in eights convinced me that to succeed in this world we must be willing to do whatever is required *despite what our mind says.* Doubts can stop us in our tracks. Thoughts can be omnipotent. Yet our thoughts have only as much power as we grant them.

It is not that doubts are wrong. Doubts are supposed to be there; they will inevitably arise. Doubt is so necessary that a Zen saying proclaims, "Small doubt, small satori, big doubt, big satori, no doubt, no satori." Our minds naturally produce an endless stream of reasons why we cannot succeed in our endeavor. And indeed, there are real obstacles between us and any prize worth pursuing.

But these obstacles are not what stop us. What stops us is getting mired in our personal mental swamps. In pursuit of a goal, we halt our own progress because we mistake our thoughts for reality. Now hear this: *thoughts are merely thoughts.* All our doubting doesn't change anything: it is just a form of wheel-spinning. The fatal trap is *entertaining* our doubts, for then we get stuck inside our own minds, insulated from the steady stream of feedback that reality is continually offering.

"Psychoanalysis is itself the disease of which it pretends to be the cure," said the Viennese aphorist Karl Kraus. We can entertain doubts for weeks, months, years; they can control our lives. In order to get free of this, we must kill this mental noise. When the impulse to entertain doubt arises, acknowledge it, then *ax it on the spot.* The moment you start feeling sorry for yourself, notice what is happening and then kill that thought. Do not "process" it, do not fight it, do not entertain it. *Kill* it.

Courage is not fearlessness, but rather the ability to take action despite one's fears. If we grapple with our fears they can immobilize us for several seconds — or a lifetime. The act of grappling keeps us stuck; as long as we are grappling with ourselves, we are prisoners, unable to move. Groups can help us stop entertaining doubts and reservations. They revoke our alumni option and so override our mind's self-sabotage. *We cannot stop rowing.*

◆

Sometimes even accountability does not reach deep enough. Once in a great while a Harvard oarsman would simply fail to show up for practice without giving notice, and there would be no spare to take his place. A crew of seven cannot row a boat and expect it to go straight. So Harry Parker himself would sit in the vacant seat and row with his crew, coaching from within the shell. On these days Parker bristled with a huge energy: his anger flared at the idea of an oarsman letting down his teammates, and Harry punished the river water for the affront. His intensity challenged everyone else in the boat to match him, and often they did; inadvertently, the marred workout would stretch the crew's capacities. The delinquent oarsman's absence changed the climate, and Parker filled the vacant space with channeled fury. Sometimes the best response to stormy weather is to unleash your own tempest. It is one way to restore equilibrium.

There are the storms that arise from the soul, and then there are those that fall on us from the skies. Inclement weather tests us: some people cancel their commitments if there is an unfavorable forecast. On fiercely rainy days, Parker would beam at his oarsmen in Newell — many of them hoping that the day's practice would be rained out — and roar, "Great day!" Rain and wind extend a superb chance to toughen ourselves, to become a notch more impervious to circumstances, to learn that we *can* perform in adverse conditions. The weather is simply another element in the equation. Every set of conditions — mirror-like, flat water on a sunny, still day or a turbulent chop stirred by nasty gusts under a darkling canopy of rain — teaches its unique lesson. *Nichi nichi kore ko nichi:* every day is a beautiful day.

The weather was challenging for the final race among eights at the 1964 Olympics in Tokyo. The showdown was between two crews of titanic ability and ambition: Ratzeburg from West Germany and the U.S. entry, Vesper Boat Club of Philadelphia. Vesper had reached the Olympics by beating Harry Parker's previously unde-feated Harvard varsity, coxed by my future coach Ted Washburn.

From 1920 to 1956, American college eights had won the gold medal at every Olympics, but in 1960 an eight that combined members of two German clubs, Kiel and Ratzeburg, won at Rome. Four years later, Vesper assembled an immensely talented group of rowers under coach Allen Rosenberg. Their talent was so deep that, had these same eight athletes been split into two fours (coxed and straight), with a subset of them also rowing in the coxed and straight pair events, they might have brought home four Olympic gold medals.

As it was, Rosenberg rounded them all up into the eight, and a contentious group it was. Fistfights sometimes broke out. An oars-man who arrived a few minutes late for practice might find a substitute already sitting in his seat and lacing up the shoes. Yet once on the water the Vesper eight was all business, showing a level of professionalism that enabled them to put aside personal ani-mosities long enough to go extremely fast.

At the Olympic trials in Pelham Bay, New York, Vesper overpow-ered the collegiate champions from Harvard and won the race by open water. After that, Harry Parker extracted a coxed four from his varsity — the boat that Washburn steered to a seventh-place finish in Tokyo. Another Harvard oarsman, Geoff Picard, eventu-ally won a bronze medal in the straight four. Vesper, however, went on to meet Ratzeburg in the eight-oared Olympic final.

Wind is enormously important in rowing. Ideal rowing weather is calm: on a still day, the water is flat, an ideal surface for rowing — uniform and predictable, with no headwind to work against. Oar-blades clear a flat surface easily. A rower's highest praise is to say that the water is "like glass," and sometimes rivers do indeed reflect like mirrors. Protected water, such as lakes nestled in valleys or streams with high banks on each side, produce flat conditions. The quest for flat water is one reason that rowers typically train early in the morning, since breezes tend to pick up as the day wears on.

But it was not calm in Tokyo for the 1964 Olympic final. During the day, a quartering wind from one side of the course had created grossly unfair conditions. In the coxed four event, the order of finish described a diagonal line across the six lanes, the lane with the most protected water winning and the windiest lane finishing last. Such an outcome is theoretically possible based on the speed of the crews, but with these particular crews that was unlikely and strongly suggested that weather conditions, rather than athletic skill, determined the results. For crews that have trained for months or years to reach this one race, such a situation is a travesty.

But sometimes the races must go on. The seven Olympic rowing events had to be completed within a prescribed period, so the officials could not wait for ideal conditions that might never arise. Thomi Keller, the head of FISA, the international governing body for rowing, postponed all the afternoon races until they could be delayed no longer. The eight-oared final race went off after dark, illuminated by flares shot into the Japanese September sky. The conditions were not unequal, but they were very difficult: on choppy water, the boats rowed directly into a howling headwind.

It may be that a rising tide raises all boats, but a headwind does not retard all boats equally. Headwinds favor muscle. Since headwinds add greatly to the effort of moving the shell forward, bigger, stronger athletes have a greater ability to pull their boats through the teeth of the gale, and for this reason beefcake crews often win in such conditions. Conversely, smaller crews, perhaps with more finesse than power, profit from a tailwind, which pushes all boats up the course faster but has a more difficult time accelerating a heavier cargo.

Both Vesper and Ratzeburg had strong crews, so a "muscle gap" did not decide the race. But while perhaps equal in bodies, they were different in their mental sets. Ratzeburg's well-protected lake, the Küchensee, offers consistently flat water for rowing — perhaps two hundred days a year of good conditions. In fact, Karl Adam believed that flat water was the only valid condition for a regatta.

Like children raised in a highly protected environment, the Ratzeburg crew found itself unprepared for harsh circumstances. They could perform at their best only when the conditions matched their preferences. But Tokyo's water was more variable than Ratzeburg's. The Vesper eight, readier for rough conditions by both training and mental set, rowed away from the Germans under the night sky and won the 1964 Olympic final by five seconds.

After their defeat, Adam and Ratzeburg declared that the race had been an invalid test due to the conditions; the Germans asserted that they were "really" faster than Vesper. In response, Vesper suggested that Ratzeburg stop denying that they had been beaten by a faster boat. The controversy grew over the next few months and climaxed in a second showdown, nine months later, at the Henley Royal Regatta in June 1965. Here the conditions were flat. The Henley format, which races only two boats at a time, made the final of the Grand Challenge Cup into a match race. Both eights went off the line at an incredible rate of 52 strokes per minute; rigged very heavily, Ratzeburg pulled out to a six-foot lead in the first ten strokes. The two great crews rowed down the course as if linked by a steel rod. Vesper almost drew even at one point but could not overtake the Germans, so Ratzeburg won by nearly half a length in a time of 6:16, which lowered the course record by seven seconds. Thus the Germans gained a measure of retribution and vindication.

Few if any endeavors proceed without some stiff headwinds. Unexpected conditions constantly arise. There are two ways to prosper in such circumstances. We can either alter the environment or find a new resource within ourselves. There is the Ratzeburg way: insist on flat water — and win there — or the Vesper way: triumph against the headwinds. Both styles can win championships, and, in daily life, most projects call for a mixture of the two strategies.

But in the long run the second option — finding a way to succeed no matter what the conditions — is the path that develops depth of character. This is the route of flexibility, the way of resourcefulness. It disciplines us to find new powers within ourselves to meet each emerging challenge. And so we grow: once developed, these new resources stay with us, enlarging our repertoire of responses, adding to the quiver of arrows we carry to meet the future. Furthermore, over time, continued success of this type builds a general sense of confidence in ourselves and our ability to handle troubles. We don't need perfect circumstances; we can thrive in any sort of weather. *Nichi nichi kore ko nichi:* every day is a beautiful day.

Resourcefulness also lets us travel lighter, since we carry our resources in ourselves rather than in our luggage. There are finicky people who fall to pieces if the weather outside is cold, or perhaps too hot, or if there is snow, sleet, rain, or wind — or if, perhaps, there are clouds in the sky. Eventually they may move to some predictable, dry climate like that of the American Southwest and, once there, spend their remaining days in air-conditioned rooms. AstroTurf and domed sports arenas enable the same flight from nature. The urge to control one's surroundings can become almost an infantile need for comfort. The need to dominate the environment eventually blocks it out, then kills it.

There are two ways to be happy. First, everyone's favorite route, Plan A: we can get what we want. Then there is Plan B: we can like what we have. Of the two, Plan B is by far the more important skill to master. First, it generates happiness right now, not in some hypothetical future when we "get what we want." Second, if we lack this skill, we won't be happy — despite our imaginings — even when we get what we want because then, *that will be what we have.* There is no future happiness.

Over my six years of rowing sweeps with Community Rowing, I saw the club grow. In traditional barn-raising style we built a boathouse, a volunteer project that involved a construction crew of elite rowers as well as beginners, pounding nails side by side. Tiff "the Hammer" Wood once again earned his nickname.

Occasionally at workouts there would be more rowers present than the coach could fit into eights, so someone would take out the club's Alden Ocean Shell. This is a very stable single, comparable to wherries but with an even wider beam. The Alden launched my career as a single sculler. Sculling a single, you set your own pace and your own course, so its lessons complement those of the eight. In singles you *can* cease to row or ease up on yourself, so they offer a way to explore your willingness to push yourself to your personal limits.

With my Alden experience behind me, I resolved to learn to row racing singles, and spent a week in June at Craftsbury Sculling Center in northern Vermont. Craftsbury's Lake Hosmer sits in a protected valley and so offers beautifully flat water. We had an intensive week of sculling instruction: there were about twenty students, several coaches, video cameras, and three coaching sessions a day.

The beginning of our first group session was actually one of the week's high points. Ostensibly it was a safety lesson on how to right a capsized single and climb back into it. Since singles are the tippiest of all shells, flipping over is a constant threat, especially for neophytes. With the entire class watching from the dock, each of us got into a single, rowed a few feet away, and intentionally capsized the boat, dumping ourselves into the water. Thus we all experienced rowing's most embarrassing mishap in full view of our fellows. But everyone had to do it. *We have all been there.*

Laughter and relief accompanied this exercise because it lightened our burdens: the worst had already happened, so we could be fearless. Furthermore, flipping the shell intentionally made capsizing a far more benign event: it was not a disaster that happened *to* us but something we had successfully accomplished. (Similarly, one therapy for stuttering is to ask someone to stutter intentionally. This subverts their resistance, and suddenly their speech is clear.)

Taking responsibility for the events that surround us generally has this salutary effect. Instead of affirming our helplessness, purposeful mishaps prove the power of our intentions. This interpretation can even work retroactively on past misfortunes that seemed unlucky. By declaring ourselves the causative agents, we regain our sense of authority — authorship — in the matter.

At Craftsbury I learned much about single sculling. The week climaxed in a race, known as the Head of the Hosmer, for all twenty students. I rowed a decent race, finishing thirteenth. Afterward, the coaches held an "awards luncheon" and gave a different prize to every participant. These trophies were uniformly trivial or eccentric (a water bottle, a bird feeder). Each prize had a ludicrous title and was bestowed with a tongue-in-cheek speech. It was an excellent ceremony for a race that included scullers at all levels of experience and ability, from teenage boys to highly competitive masters women to sexagenarian men. It underscored the fact that ultimately we row only against ourselves, and the clock.

Soon I found myself in another head race, at the other extreme of the sport: the 1986 Head of the Charles Regatta. That was the summer that Tom Tiffany and I were accepted in the Championship Doubles event, when I rowed briefly with Tiff Wood, and when Tom and I sporadically trained in the old Pocock "tub."

By race day we had secured a better shell, a Kaschper double. However, while we both had rowed in various sweep and sculling boats all summer long, neither of us had done anything resembling serious training. We had rowed the double no more than a dozen times. Even if we had trained hard, Tom and I would have finished quite far back in the Championship Doubles, an open event that attracts some of the world's fastest scullers. We were like club tennis players signing up for the doubles draw at Wimbledon. Tom and I were essentially novice scullers — undertrained beginners, of no great size and only average talent.

Nonetheless, on this sunny October afternoon in 1986, we feel good as we row our Kaschper to the starting line. The racing conditions are excellent. Tom and I start strongly, giving it everything we have, but even so, other shells begin hurtling past us in short order. We start well back in the pack, and by the one-mile mark we have a firm grip on last place: the river is all ours. Since the Head is a race against the clock, we cannot know how we will do until the race is over, but even at this point a last-place finish looks well within our grasp.

Tom, an international-caliber coxswain, steers and rows bow while I stroke the boat. Consequently we row an excellent course, even if we are spending an exceptional amount of time doing so. By the one-mile mark of this three-mile race I am already tired out and realize I will have to bull through the last two miles. Then I get a second wind. As the race wears on, cycles of collapse and renewal repeat themselves; I get third and then fourth winds. I think: *this is too many winds.* We reach the two-mile mark, and although I know perfectly well where we are, I gaspingly ask Tom how far we have to go: oxygen debt has reduced me to irrationality. He answers that we have "only" a mile left. *Don't* tell *me that this isn't the finish line,* I think. *This has* got *to be the finish line; I am already on my fourth wind and there is no way I can row another hundred feet, let alone another mile.* Yet somehow we do row that last mile and finish the race. I don't know about Tom, but I have accomplished the impossible — several times over. Never mind that we were amazingly slow: we did it.

When the results go up, we find that we have indeed nailed down last place. We were not, however, the slowest boat on the river today, just the slowest one in our event. To say we were "outclassed" in the Championship Doubles is a severe understatement, though literally correct: we were in the wrong class. Tom and I were trying to do something we were not remotely prepared for. As we paddle downstream after the race, a coach from M.I.T. tosses us a couple cans of beer to enhance our trip back to the dock. "Well, this shows what we need to do next time," I tell Tiffany after a refreshing sip. "Train."

That day there were entries who never started the race and others who never finished. But we went the distance. Despite burning lungs and muscles that said *no more,* we kept pushing upstream. *Don't take No for an answer.* Years later, I learned that elite rowers had these same feelings — lungs on fire, muscles saying *we must stop now* — only they experienced these sensations at higher boat speeds. The pain is always there, waiting for us at the perimeter of our capacities, wherever that horizon may fall. Yet, steadily pushing through that pain gradually expands those capacities. And hence we train.

Why did we not train more? The simple answer is that Tom and I both had other commitments and didn't assign a high priority to race preparation. To me, rowing was then a recreational activity, not a competitive one. For the others it was different; with few exceptions, our competitors had trained hard to race, and their diligence paid off in boat speed. Eventually I, too, would follow that path of disciplined training and reap its rewards. But in my second year of rowing, it was a triumph simply to finish the three miles of the Head of the Charles.

The race left satisfactions and interesting questions in its wake. I had learned something of what I could and could not do and got a sense of my place in the rowing hierarchy: at the bottom of the totem pole, to be exact. Yet our lack of experience, training, and coaching kept open the question of how well I might do if I actually prepared for a race.

For the next few years I continued sweep rowing, and then, after 1990, moved almost exclusively to sculling boats. As my professional life became more demanding, single sculling was the practical alternative, largely because singles offer more scheduling flexibility. It would be several more years before I again tested myself in a big race, risking my self-concept to find out who I really was in this world and on this river. Perhaps the great Head of the Charles Regatta might still hold an answer to the mystery that had stayed with me since childhood: *Am I a real athlete?*

Answering this riddle would mean that, like Caesar, I would have to burn some of the ships that had kept me afloat. There would be disciplines to master, and I would have to outgrow habits and comforts that were woven into my life. In essence, the challenge was to create a new identity, one that would support a higher velocity afloat.

Speed comes at a price. Getting fast on the water can create imbalances on land, straining finances, jobs, marriages. In this world, nothing is free: to create, one must be willing to destroy. We paint over canvases, tear up first drafts, rearrange boatings for the varsity crew. Doing this hurts. But creation moves forward like a sailboat tacking toward a port; without some element of revision and destruction, the boat is in irons. Life burns hottest at the edge of loss. When death flirts with us, our skin tingles and reminds us of how alive we are *now*.

Unless we destroy muscle tissue, we cannot build muscles. Growth takes place at the perimeter of possibility. By testing a muscle to its limits, we break down its fibers — but the body recovers, renewing the destroyed fibers and growing even more tissue to meet the heightened level of demand.

Thus we gain muscular strength by exercising to failure, to the point where we cannot lift the weight again. Without failure there is no progress. Say we can bench-press 150 pounds and do ten repetitions ("reps") of that lift. If we continue to perform ten reps at that weight, we will maintain the strength we have but won't increase it. The eleventh rep produces results. That last rep is by far the most painful one, since it asks our body to do more than it can — that is, to expand its possibilities. We doubt whether our muscles can really make the eleventh rep — but somehow do it anyway. The eleventh rep is an act of will.

In the shadowy area between mind and body, between character and muscle fiber, between thoughts and brain chemistry, we discover the power to create reality. The physical body incarnates what the soul asks. Thoughts become tissue. In the penumbra of the human spirit we enter a zone of pain and divine powers.

Rowing is an attempt at mastery. Every workout confronts us with our doubts. We try something we think we cannot do. With discipline, we may demonstrate that in fact *we can do it*. Uncertainty can actually be a fuel; the greater the doubt, the greater the will required to overcome it. Furthermore, when an experiment in defeating doubt succeeds, it shakes the very foundations of doubting. If we go beyond what we once thought was our perimeter, then all limits are open to question. We row toward an ever-expanding horizon.

To compete and to create: the dialectic of birth and destruction. Two primal forces spiral together in the deepest mysteries, where love and death intersect, in art, in sex, in athletics. They vie with each other, even as they beget the future: the painting not yet seen, the child waiting to be born, the race we are about to row.

The Powerhouse Stretch

What you don't bet is what you lose,
when you win.

— FLIP WILSON

To OUR PORT SIDE, the powerhouse abides in majesty. Four strips of color — yellow, blue, green, red, as in *wood, water, grass, brick* — form a spectrum that links us. From beneath the bridge, we row into splendor as the setting sun fires the river with magenta and flames of gold. Tall smokestacks rise from the powerhouse and waft plumes of smoke into the sky, the epitaph of fuel burned into power. Rowers call this reach of the Charles River the powerhouse stretch; it is a straightaway about 1,000 meters long where boats can attain maximum speed. Many races have occurred here. Invoking the word *powerhouse* has been known, all by itself, to bring forth speed in a crew.

This evening I sit in the center of the boat, in the #5 seat. We are easing comfortably into our warm-up. The ritual evokes a meditative state. Deep breaths infuse oxygen into my blood, then blood into tissues, awakening muscles and memories. It is always thus. The first hundred strokes stretch limbs out, loosening tendons and connecting me with other times on the river. To starboard, another eight paddles downstream. Soon we will have at each other.

Before a race, even a scrimmage, there is always anxiety. It is essential. If there is no fear, we don't have enough at stake. *Gamble more than you can afford to lose, and you just might win.* Tonight we have a secret weapon: the calm, assured voice of our coxswain, a former member of the U.S. national team, quiets our nerves like a seasoned airline pilot explaining the flight plan as we taxi out to the runway. His confidence becomes our own.

On the water, though, it is ultimately the stroke who is in charge. When in doubt, we follow the stroke's blade, not the cox's voice. If the cox orders the rate up two but the stroke stands pat, the rate will *not* go up. While the coxswain's power is *de jure,* the stroke rules *de facto.* Luckily, strokes rarely overrule their steersmen. Stroke and cox are the only two crew members who face each other, and they had better see eye to eye. Should they disagree often, the boat is in trouble. Tonight, happily, it feels like stroke, cox, and the rest of the crew are on the same wavelength.

In front of Riverside Boat Club, we turn around to head upstream. Our coach brings the two eights together, lines us up, and tells us we'll row for three minutes and see which boat is ahead. Then he announces, "Ready all? Row!" and our scrimmage race starts. Our boat gets off well, and after thirty strokes we are a seat up.

Something happens as we emerge from the River Street Bridge and come up on the red brick powerhouse. "Now, the powerhouse stretch," our cox intones. "So *feel* that power *now* . . . staying long . . . We're going up two, *in* two . . . Now *watch* us . . . *one* . . . *two* . . . on *this* one!" Tumblers fall into place — *click* — and a lock opens. Suddenly the boat gets quiet; we hear only eight oars grabbing the water together, finishing as one. Some energy flow grips us like a river current, synchronizing our motion; we row as one body. Thinking disappears, leaving behind only presence and rhythm; yes, presence and rhythm are rowing this boat, using us for oars.

The boat is perfectly level. Set up beautifully, we skim the surface on an invisible laser beam running from horizon to horizon. There is no friction; we ride the natural cadence of our strokes, a continuous cycle. The crew breathes as one. Inhale on the recovery, exhale as we drive our blades through the water: inspiration and expression. *In. Out.* Row with one body and so with one mind. Nothing exists but: *Here. Now. This.* Rushing water bubbles under our hull, as if a mountain brook buried within the Charles flows directly beneath us. I have never heard this sound before, but I know that it means we are doing something right.

The coach calls the end of our three-minute piece and we gradually come out of the trance. Back on earth, I recall that we were racing, and wonder what happened to the other boat, which is nowhere in sight. Then I see them, a hundred yards downstream, a good five boat lengths behind us. We must have horizoned them.

Rowers have a word for this frictionless state: *swing.* "On the third piece we really started swinging," someone will say, or, "We tried a new lineup in the four and it just didn't swing." Swing is the coveted, effortless condition where everything falls into place. In some ways it resembles "the zone," a personal transcendent state, but it also opens up realms beyond any personal zones. It is, in fact, zoneless. The experience of swing is what hooks people on rowing: they seek to recapture that lucid state again and again. The appetite for swing is limitless.

Recall the pure joy of riding on a backyard swing: an easy cycle of motion, the momentum coming from the swing itself. The swing carries us; we do not force it. We pump our legs to drive our arc higher, but gravity does most of the work. We are not so much swinging as being swung.

The boat swings you. The shell wants to move fast: speed sings in its lines and nature. Our job is simply to work with the shell, to stop holding it back with our thrashing struggles to go faster. Trying too hard sabotages boat speed. Trying becomes striving, and striving undoes itself. Social climbers strive to be aristocrats, but their efforts prove them no such thing. Aristocrats do not strive; they have already arrived. Swing is a state of arrival.

On crews, some rowers are called *anchors,* human impedimenta who slow down boats. Anchors lack grace, partly because they try to do it all themselves. The isolated mentality cuts supply lines: it blocks supportive energies from boat, oars, teammates, opponents, spectators, and the forces of nature. Anchors set up an ongoing struggle of self versus environment. Disconnected individuals do not swing.

Swing taps lodes of energy, entraining us with primal rhythms. Swing *is* rhythm — a mode of self-transcendence or, more accurately, an expanded definition of self. On the powerhouse stretch, the state of swing redefined "me," as on that Saturday years before, when wind and water taught me to sail. As the boat swings, my identity dissolves, reconfigures, and I become the shell's vehicle, the instrument of swing.

The male organism evolved to compete, and so we males constantly seek victories. Our bodies' evolution reflects the role men played as warriors/protectors of prehistoric clans: bigger bones and muscles, testosterone, aggression, a tendency to violence. All of these once aided survival, particularly when hunting. Today they have outlived much of their adaptive value. Yet they are still useful in certain venues, such as the military, corporate life, and in sports.

Females do not lack instincts for rivalry. The Darwinian imperatives of survival apply to both sexes: women, too, have strong competitive drives. But women's contests usually have a different flavor, one that stresses outdoing opponents rather than destroying them.

Consider that prehistoric peoples were hunter-gatherers: males hunted animals and females gathered plant foods. Gathering involves competition with other species and other humans. But a gathering expedition is a less mortal occasion than a hunt: stalking prehistoric prey often meant killing the prey or being killed. Meanwhile other predators were stalking *Homo sapiens,* giving the male hunter the bracing double role of hunter and prey. One had to be quiet: the "strong, silent type" perhaps evolved as a survival strategy.

As a hunter in the mid-twentieth century, from my earliest years I sought to win. In part, my competitive nature drove the diligent schoolwork that kept me at the top of my class. Winning meant straight As on report cards and dominating academic competitions. Often it simply meant being the only student who knew the right answer to a teacher's question: it was especially gratifying to answer correctly after several other students had tried and failed. To win required that someone else lose.

As a boy I played team sports, so it was more difficult to stand out as a winner. There were only a few moments when I could star. But when my team won, the joy of victory was delicious. Winning absolved all the errors we had made during the game: those mistakes obviously didn't matter much, since we had won. Dazzled by the outcome, we erased the process that led to it. But losing a contest was very different; it deepened the anguish of every miscue. Regret stuck to those errors, because without them we might have won.

From early youth I was also an avid spectator. I rooted for my high school and college teams and closely followed professional sports as a partisan fan of the Brooklyn (later Los Angeles) Dodgers in baseball, the New York Giants in football , and in basketball, the most successful pro sports franchise of my lifetime, the Boston

Celtics. Later, when I moved to Boston, I added the Red Sox. In front of the television set, I was deeply engaged: clapping, yelling, complaining, growling, laughing with my father, my brother, or my male friends, and even a few female ones. If my team won, it validated my judgment, my beliefs, my values. Victory affirmed that I was on the right side and that what I cherished — the soulfulness and foibles of the Dodgers, say, compared to the humorless, mechanical New York Yankees — was the path of honor.

In contrast, losing deflated the ego and hurt deeply. Sometimes I wondered how I could experience such deep misery over the fate of a handful of men whom I did not know, playing a game against another group of strangers in a ballpark hundreds of miles away. The answer was simple: I loved my teams. Although risky, caring was worth its price. Sports fired up my blood, excited me, made my heart pound. I liked having something at stake. Life was more vivid during a contest.

In adult life, as I took up individual sports, my competitive instincts expressed themselves in varied ways. In 5- or 10-kilometer foot races I had modest expectations: I often ran alongside a friend and was content to complete the race, paying little attention to my time. Before starting, I knew that the vast majority would finish before me.

However, even at the rear of the pack, one beats a few competitors. On assignment for *Sports Illustrated,* I once ran the 7.1-mile Falmouth Road Race in Falmouth, Massachusetts, alongside Ruth Rothfarb. At eighty-nine, Ruth was the oldest competitive female athlete alive. To stay with her, I had to slow even my own modest pace, and we finished very far back indeed. Yet, afterward, as we stood drinking bottled water in an open field, Ruth pointed out a long line of runners still on the course, trudging toward the finish line. "See, they're still coming in," she said, smiling. Yes, we had beaten some people.

Such moments ask us to reconsider the meaning of winning. Our culture seems to view winning as an absolute: in every sport there is only one ultimate winner — the World Series champion, the Super Bowl victors, the NBA titlists. *In this country, you're either #1 or you're nothing.* But consider one such pinnacle, the Wimbledon tennis tournament. Winning Wimbledon is a tremendous achievement and resoundingly demonstrates one's mastery of tennis. But on the first day, the gentlemen's singles draw includes 128 players, and there are 128 more in the ladies' draw. Two weeks later, one man and one woman emerge as champions, each leaving 127 losers in their wake. However, these "losers" are the finest tennis players in the world, athletes who could win 99 percent of the tennis tournaments played, even giving all comers a 4–0 handicap in each set. Some losers.

Dave Fish, one of my tennis coaches, once told me he had found a secret that would guarantee that I would win every match I played. The secret, he said, was playing opponents who were under five or over ninety years of age. "You'll win every time," Dave said. "Satisfied?"

Fish wanted me to ask myself what I was really seeking on the court. He was also showing that the value of competition depends on an even match. The game is exciting only when we can imagine both contestants having a chance to win. Hence all the class divisions in sport: age categories, men's and women's sports, weight classes in boxing and rowing, colored belts in karate, boat classes in sailing. By controlling certain factors, the game asks not simply who can win, but who can do the best with comparable resources. Given the cards you hold, how well can you play?

Consequently, losing stings less when you are competing out of your class. When Tom and I finished dead last in the Head of the Charles, I did not take the loss very hard. For one thing, there was the simple justice of the verdict: everyone else trained harder than we did, and everyone else went faster than we did. Second, most of our competitors were bigger than we were. Third, neither of us had done that much sculling; we had stumbled into a Championship (open) event by accident, so to stumble through it and out of it actually seemed fitting. We did not fall short of any lofty goals. We were beginners, outclassed by the best in the sport.

On the tennis court I gave myself less latitude for failure. Like many tennis players, I failed to understand that execution is a batting average. If, for example, I could recall successfully hitting a backhand approach shot down the line, I concluded that *I can make this shot.* Consequently, hitting such a shot wide, long, or into the net was frustrating because I had just blown a shot I knew I could make. What I failed to consider was probability. Yes, I can make that shot, *but only about 20 percent of the time.* Perhaps a pro can execute the same shot (with more power and spin) 90 percent of the time. Irrationally, I was expecting myself to perform flawlessly 100 percent of the time. Every error felt like a failure to do something that was — I thought — well within my capacities.

Even small improvements in one's percentage of success can produce spectacular results. Consider major league baseball, where someone with a .250 batting average is a journeyman, a .300 batter is a fine player, and a .350 hitter is a superstar. Assume 500 at-bats a season. Using that denominator, a .250 average calls for 125 hits; .300 means 150 hits, and .350 requires 175 hits. But the baseball season, stretching from April through September, is roughly twenty-five weeks long. Hence the difference between an average player and a standout is *one more hit a week,* and superstardom is only two hits away. If a team plays six games weekly, resulting in 24 at-bats, the shift from mediocrity to greatness involves simply moving from 6 to 8 hits. In fact, most .250 hitters do have weeks in which they hit safely eight times or even more. But the batting champion performs at that level *every single week.* Success in sports, as elsewhere, is no big thing: it is every little thing, achieved on a daily basis.

In endurance sports like rowing, coaches emphasize building up vast reserves of aerobic stamina. It may take a young rower five years to reach full aerobic capacity, which helps explain why few perform at world-class levels before their early twenties. Well-trained competitors also cultivate mental toughness, which enables them to get the most from those aerobic reserves. But even such thorough training confines us to personal capacities of mind and body: yes, we can increase endurance and strength, but only to the limits that our individual organism allows.

Philosophy, said Wittgenstein, *is simply showing the fly the way out of the bottle.* One way out of this confining bottle is the Chinese concept of Qi (pronounced *chee*), which takes us beyond individual effort. Qi is cosmic energy, a force of nature, a wellspring whose origin is radically impersonal. Qi fuels not only human organisms but the solar wind, the orbits of stars and planets, magnetic fields. Hence it frees us from the separated ego, the skin-bound organism. The athlete who taps into Qi vaults beyond the limits of physical tissues and mental states into a constantly recharging power source.

Early in my career as a runner I experienced Qi. One beautiful September day I went out for an easy run around Fresh Pond in Cambridge, a route I could then complete in about twenty minutes. But after one lap around the pond I still felt strong, and it was a lovely day to be outdoors. I decided to continue. Not long into my second lap, running somehow turned into an effortless process. It felt as if my body were made of flexible rubber. I was no longer transporting myself with my legs; instead, it seemed my whole body was running. More accurately, it felt as if I were being run —

that "running" had taken me over for its own purposes. Furthermore, the exertion did not feel like exertion: it was not costing me anything to run: the process was so frictionless that each stride subtracted nothing from my energy resources. Rather, I drew on some infinite energy account that was continually refilled. I felt as if I could run forever, even after having kept a steady pace for over an hour.

Albert Einstein remarked that we cannot solve any problem on the level of thinking where it was created. Qi is a concept that may eventually shatter the current paradigms of coaching, producing the next breakthrough in athletic performance. Qi opens up an impersonal source of energy beyond the limits of body and mind — accessed, perhaps, not by effort, but by presence and rhythm.

The quality of presence relates to our capacity to dwell in the here-and-now, to inhabit the *present*. We accomplish this by letting go of distractions — by quieting the mind, as in meditation. The settled state lets us embrace the moment, with its complex chord of sensory inputs. Thus we leave our thoughts and enter the world, in a state of heightened attention — increased presence — that opens a channel to Qi.

In sports, Qi correlates with a sense of limitless capacity, a feeling that we can do whatever we set our minds to. Hence visualizations — images of ourselves executing ideal performances — can help us find Qi. Such images design the condition we intend to create; without a clear model, we produce chaotic results. Visualizations offer a mold, so to speak, into which Qi may flow.

Qi has rhythm. When we align ourselves with wider rhythms, we open a channel to its flow. By entraining ourselves with the cadences that surround us, we escape our separated individuality and swim from a pool of energy into an ocean.

A few years ago I took a long bicycle ride on Martha's Vineyard by myself. It was late on a summer afternoon, and the roads were unusually deserted. A dark sky with a towering thunderhead loomed ahead of me, and I realized I would need to make excellent time in order to get home before the storm hit.

I became centered on one task: forging ahead on my bicycle at the maximum safe speed I could sustain. Before long my breathing fell into a regular cadence, as if I were conducting music in 4/4 time. I entered a breath cycle with a downbeat to start each measure: 1-2-3-4, 1-2-3-4. That was on flat terrain. Heading downhill, I kept my speed constant, but my breathing shifted to a 3/4 time signature, still accented on the first beat: 1-2-3, 1-2-3. Then, going uphill, I began breathing in 6/8, exhaling harder on the first and fourth breaths: 1-2-3-4-5-6, 1-2-3-4-5-6.

It dawned on me that I was breathing with the landscape; actually, the terrain was breathing me. The island and I kept to a single rhythm. Having learned this lesson, I could later let the running path I ran, or the water I rowed, control my breathing. Qi infuses all of our surroundings; it is always there, ready for us to find it.

I joined my rowing club, Cambridge Boat Club, in 1988. Many elite rowers, either in or near their competitive primes, gravitate toward Cambridge, a haven for scullers, where the atmosphere offers both competition and camaraderie. I also affiliated myself with CRASH-B, an acronym for the Charles River Association of Sculling Has-Beens, a ragtag bunch of former rowing greats plus a few not-so-greats, like myself. Tiff Wood enrolled me in the group despite my protest that I could not be a Sculling Has-Been since I had never Been.

Nonetheless I joined the regatta committee for CRASH-B's annual rowing machine competition, known as the CRASH-B Sprints or World Indoor Rowing Championships. Each February since 1982, the Sprints had attracted top rowers to compete on Concept-II ergometers. The ergs' electronic performance monitors, which precisely measure time elapsed and "distance" rowed, make it possible to stage a race on rowing machines.

Although it is a serious athletic competition, CRASH-B never took itself too seriously. For example, the race program's list of CRASH-B officers included a "chaplain," Hartley Rogers, an M.I.T. mathematics professor with no theological training whatever. Each year before the CRASH-B finals, Peter Raymond, an Olympic silver medalist, strode out in black tie and bowler to play "The Star-Spangled Banner" on solo violin. Raymond was a supremely inept violinist who had never taken a lesson: the CRASH-B board of directors enhanced his dissonance by voting to prohibit him from practicing. Raymond's performance was excruciating, and the enthusiastic cheers at the anthem's conclusion were even more heartfelt than usual, though for a different reason.

I could not miss out on this kind of inspired buffoonery and so signed on to help the CRASH-B regatta committee with publicity. My biggest coup came in 1987, when I wrote and published an article on the event in *Sports Illustrated*. Again, as part of my research, I entered as a competitor.

In some ways, rowing the ergometer closely resembles rowing a shell. Ergs simulate the rowing stroke and train muscles and physiology for some of the demands of real rowing. But indoor rowing omits much of the complexity of rowing on water, such as blade-work, balancing the shell, and adapting to conditions like wind and powerboat wakes. Technique plays a much smaller role on the erg. Ergs are to rowing as the skiing machine is to cross-country skiing — the basic motion and muscular work are there, but no snow.

Rowing machines do offer exact data. The Concept-II's performance monitor computes stroke rate, time elapsed, split times for 500 meters, and an equivalent "distance rowed" in meters. At the CRASH-B finals, a video monitor translates this information into a display of six lanes of boats. The "boats" inch along a video course in direct response to each athlete's efforts — allowing a visual simulation of a race.

For the athlete, the erg's exact readouts are a blessing and a curse. The blessing is that a split time on the monitor offers a benchmark for measuring performance. That is also the curse. The satanic monitor delivers ruthlessly accurate information on every single stroke. There is no way to fool yourself: if your last stroke was even a tenth of a second off your targeted pace, the monitor lets you know instantly. This can be discouraging. There is such a thing as being overinformed.

Rowing coaches use erg scores to evaluate athletes; they are one way to identify the most physically fit specimens. The erg is a physiological instrument. If a 2:00 split time represents your fastest possible pace for a 2,000-meter distance, you will hit a *steel wall* at 1:59 — you *cannot* row the race at 1:59. Few things in life are this absolute. Uninitiated spectators sometimes remark, "Gee, if you had only 'gone for it' a bit more, just one second faster each split, you'd have come in at 7:56 and moved up eighty-five places in the world rankings!" *But I could have just as easily stood the Statue of Liberty on its head as taken another second off those splits.* The erg is a pure test of our ability to inhale oxygen, burn it, and convert the result into physical work. Our bodies set certain outer limits where we really do have to take No for an answer.

At least for today. Over longer periods of time we can expand those limits, and so we train. By asking our cells to do more than they are used to doing, we coax our bodies into catching up with our desires. We can grow new capillaries and open up the ones we have, add muscle tissue, slow down our heart rates, pump blood more efficiently.

With any luck we also lose weight, trimming our body-fat percentage. As I trained through the winter of 1987, I did indeed burn fat; my weight and erg times plummeted together. But another problem remained: could I survive CRASH-B?

That year, the race distance was 2,500 meters (today it is 2,000). Over the winter I had gradually whittled down my 2,500-meter time from well over eleven minutes to a personal best of 10:45. This was not world-class, national-class, or even metropolitan-class rowing. In a nutshell, it was not class rowing. As a benchmark, the open record was 7:27, and the world record for men in my age group (30–39) was 7:40; finishing three minutes after the leaders is definitely quite far back. Again I lagged on the training curve; by race day in mid-February, I would have been training seriously for only two months. Dedicated rowers, of course, train year-round, and some start preparing for the Sprints in the early fall. At least my eight weeks had been systematic ones.

In the heart of February, around Valentine's Day, the river ice is thick enough to walk on; we can at last walk to Boston from Cambridge without a bridge. On race day, one oarsman tells me of a bet he's made with a friend: the guy with the slower time has to chop a hole in the ice and stand in the freezing water for ten seconds. "Even that will be painless," he says, "after CRASH-B."

Yes, the erg race hurts: like any regatta, it asks you to go all out. Unfortunately, with the erg there is nothing to distract you from the pain. Today I will be tested. Inside the regatta site, a huge gym at M.I.T., several hundred energetic, keyed-up people in superb physical condition mill around. Heats begin at 8:00 A.M.; mine goes off at 9:50.

My race plan is simple. Since my personal best is 10:45, I will aim to repeat that by rowing five 500-meter splits at 2:09 each. Even splits are a generally sound strategy in races of this type, and with the meter giving constant readouts, there is no real excuse for not pacing myself. Fifty brand-new Concept-IIs are whirring around me in the gym at 9:45 as I tighten the straps that hold my feet down. I have already warmed up on another erg in the practice area. I adjust the vent on the side of the machine to its midpoint, giving the level of resistance I prefer. Then race assistants come around and staunch all the flywheels with their palms. The gym gets quieter. The starter raises a flag above his head: just like outdoors, the race starts when that flag swoops down, with the irrevocability of a guillotine — but instead of ending all pain, this stroke begins it. I compress my body, poised at the catch for the first stroke, until the starter drones the then-standard international starting commands through the bullhorn: "*Êtes-vous prets? Partez!*"

I am off. For the first minute I feel like Superman: it is always so. Drawing on that lode of anaerobic energy, for the first thirty strokes I can drive the meter under 2:00 until reality obtrudes and the numbers slip up to the 2:09 neighborhood, where I plan to race. I take full advantage of this early burst since these stronger strokes will create a hedge against slow spells later in the race, when I may find my numbers floating above 2:09.

I settle into my racing cadence, aiming to lock the merciless monitor onto that 2:09 split time. This is not an especially pleasant task. But it is something I know I can do. In an erg race, we have a very clear idea of what our capacities are, so racing becomes a question of actualizing them. This is reassuring, but less fun than *not* knowing what you can do, rowing into a mystery that the race eventually resolves.

Yet I may be deceived. Maybe, as in tennis, I am expecting to play my best game every day, consistently repeating my best performance. Is the erg piece more like being asked to breathe twenty times a minute — an activity I know I can replicate — or is it like executing a backhand approach shot down the line? There is a reason, after all, why my 10:45 time is a personal *best:* I have achieved it only once. Though the erg is a machine, I am not.

The image of the human body as a machine gained favor as the Industrial Revolution placed machinery in the forefront of Western consciousness. As machines fascinated, seduced, and eventually shaped our society, we came to view our bodies as another mechanical device. Medical doctors described hearts, livers, blood vessels, and nerves as components of a mechanism called the body. Nutritionists compared the body to an automobile, which needs good fuel to run well. With the spread of mass production and interchangeable parts, medicine extended the machine analogy, and surgeons began to transplant hearts, livers, and kidneys from one person into another, like replacement parts.

The transition from the Industrial Age to the Information Age brought a new set of metaphors into vogue. Now medicine describes DNA as coded information, data for the body's calculations. Scientists tell us that the brain is like a biological computer, essentially an information-processing device. Our neurons are switches, and thinking is a type of software.

No doubt these technological concepts can help scientists organize and communicate their findings. But the body spurns them, just as it rejects organ transplants. Nature bristles against transplants with an immune response that only more technology, in the form of powerful drugs, can quash. The brain is no computer, any more than the ocean is a glass of water. True, they both contain H_2O, but the oceans, with their lunar tides, reefs, plant and animal life, depths, waves, and ever-changing colors, mock any such comparison.

These reductive analogies exact a fearsome price from the human soul. If we believe our bodies to be machines and our brains to be computers, we will wonder why we do not function with mechanistic consistency. *I should perform perfectly 100 percent of the time.* Humanity becomes a case of defective technology. We feel flawed since we lack the reliability of the inanimate world; what is alive fails by comparison to that which is not.

Real, living bodies and minds change, grow, and decline. We have good and bad days. In weight training I do not progress uniformly, always lifting more and more weight on a given exercise. On some days, mysteriously, I simply cannot lift as much as I did a week before, even though my general trend over the weeks and months is consistently upward. The body is not a machine; it is what created machinery.

Hence imponderables persist. As I race at CRASH-B, I don't know whether I will even be able to go as fast as I have in most recent workouts — around 10:50. During a race, energy levels ebb and flow, sometimes quite randomly. Five minutes into the race, for no particular reason, I get a second wind. I am opportunistic with this bonus and capitalize by rowing near 2:00 for as long as the tailwind holds. But as the minutes slip by, the buildup of lactic acid in my tissues — a by-product of exercise —- creates pervasive aching through my body. After about 8:00 elapsed, a patch of fatigue nudges my numbers up: 2:10, 2:11, 2:13. This is where the mind has to take control: *don't take No for an answer.* I quite literally dig in my heels on the foot stretchers and concentrate on keeping my stroke long, riding out the energy valley until normal strength returns.

Which it does. At the start of the race, the monitor read 2,500 meters. Depending on its power, each stroke trims a few meters from that total, and the display shows the ever-declining distance left to row. In the last 200 meters I have enough left for a finishing sprint, so I take my rate up to 36 and go out strong. At the finish, the distance remaining finally reads 0.00, and my time is 10:41.3.

Not bad for a working journalist, I think, recalling how a crew coach once told me, You'll win a lot more medals as a writer than you ever will as an oarsman. My time, nearly four seconds below my previous personal best, surprises me. I wonder if the charged atmosphere in the room, the stimulus of competition, somehow seeped into my body and drove me faster than I had ever gone. *The crew makes the individual shine.* Something must have reached me, an extra charge of energy. I rowed fairly even splits, a steady pace that realized my maximum output. There was nothing left over at the end. *What you don't bet is what you lose, when you win.*

Still, I am less willing to endure pain than some. At the end of the 2,500-meter piece, a few rowers roll off their seats, collapsing onto the floor. If they were not superbly conditioned athletes, we might fear for their lives. One elite oarswoman noticed that her thighs had turned blue, presumably a consequence of blood having withdrawn from the skin in order to keep more essential organs alive during her finishing sprint. Another lost most of her hearing for twenty minutes after the race. My exertions did not reach these levels, but I am satisfied. Today, I rowed my race.

Numerical data are especially useful when we have to make a decision but doubt our judgment. When we don't trust ourselves, we lean on the numbers: Nielsen ratings, earnings reports, research polls, ergometer scores. We can defend our conclusions by citing the "hard" data we based them on. *The blood counts and chest x-ray looked good. How was I supposed to know he had lung cancer?* In contrast, when we use our instincts and intuition, we alone are responsible for the decision we make.

Captivated by numbers, we resemble obsessive-compulsive personalities: obsessed with thoroughness and getting everything precisely right, we have little room for intuition. We become like airplane pilots flying on instruments — altimeter, air speed, compass heading. The instruments do indeed produce the numbers and a way to navigate. But with our eyes on the dials, we never look outside the cockpit. Glued to the screen, we miss what is happening.

In a culture addicted to winning, we tend to focus on the final score. The ultimate verdict is all that matters unless you are a gambler with a point spread — and even then, the focus is on the score. In rowing there is no scoreboard, but there are race times, and there are surely wins and losses. As my sculling career progressed, I gradually recognized that while I had relished my athletic wins, they were not what most satisfied me.

What hooked me on athletics were certain feelings, sights, and sounds — sensual delights. The way it feels to stride into a fastball, hear the melodious *craack* of a wooden bat connecting solidly, then see a line drive sail into the gap between left and center field. The trajectory of a golf drive, a low takeoff that rises, bisecting the fairway, then fades. The brush of a basketball swishing through the strings of the net. *All net.* A tennis ball's deep-pitched *thwock*, the graceful arc of a backhand passing shot ripping crosscourt and touching down briefly near the singles sideline before it kicks away.

I loved the languid feel of water against oar. With delicious viscosity, water resists the blade even as it surrenders, a combination that offers the perfect counterpoise to one's muscles. With the blade submerged, you need not even sit on the seat — you are suspended in midair, feet pushing against the foot stretchers, hands hooked around the oar handle, blade anchored in the river. On a good stroke you *hang* on the water. Rowing engages the whole body, fully immerses it in each stroke. Facing astern, we cannot view our forward trajectory, but we are compensated by the symmetry of our wake.

Such pleasures spring from feelings, sounds, sights. Everyone who plays a sport, at whatever level of ability, can taste these moments. Certainly talent, coaching, and experience can multiply such rewards and also open new sensory realms available only to the advanced athlete. Yet these visceral delights do not require expertise, nor do they depend on competition or winning. These experiences are senior to the score. In a sense, they constitute the only guaranteed way to win, no matter when we cross the finish line.

"Rowing is not a game," a British coach once noted, adding that "the dictionary will not let you either play or play at rowing." It can, however, be a diversion: on some days I have simply paddled on the stream like Thoreau, inhaling the scent of cold spring air, dawdling along to notice buds opening, a heron posing near the shore, a cormorant's swoop to the water, duck fledglings swimming in single file behind their parents.

Yet the boat is a jealous mistress, calling for my attention and involvement. Something about the simplicity of the rowing stroke or the shape of the shell, so desirous of speed, compels us to perfect our oarsmanship, to row with elegance and effect. I am also blessed (or perhaps cursed) with ambition. For me it is impossible to row along placidly forever without testing myself. Tests can be benchmarks, like rowing a 500-meter erg piece in under 1:50. But they can also be subjective or even social. In my case, one milestone I sought was meeting some tribal standard, to earn a valid place in the rowing community.

And so in the summer of 1995 I mailed an entry form to the Head of the Charles. At forty-seven I qualified for the men's Senior Masters Single race, for oarsmen from forty to forty-nine. Because the Head is so celebrated, competitive, and prestigious, it attracts far more applicants than it can accept. Aside from single scullers and crews who have proven their speed in previous years, applicants enter a lottery that accepts only a small fraction as competitors. To my surprise, I was one of them.

I had been training a fair amount that year, so I had a running start. Yet now that I was in the Big Show, I would have to ratchet up my efforts, mobilizing on several fronts. The first item was setting my goal. I knew at the outset that I would not finish near the top of the pack, nor crack the top half of the draw. For one thing, as the baby-boom generation has entered its middle years in the last two decades, masters rowing has grown dramatically, and masters races have become far more competitive. Winning times in open events have begun to converge with those in the over-forty, over-fifty, and over-sixty categories. This is largely because the older athletes are getting much faster. Most of the men in my race would be training ferociously all year round and would have been sculling competitively for years. Most were big guys. Some had been national champions or world-class oarsmen a few years back and were still in great shape. In no way was my speed going to approach that of the vast majority of entrants.

I set a more attainable goal: to finish within the "normal" range. My objective was to prepare as thoroughly as possible and see whether I could legitimately be part of the field at a high-level athletic event. I knew that my time would fall at the tail end of the normal curve, but for me it would be a meaningful achievement just to be on the curve rather than off it; I didn't want to be an "outlier." In the Championship Doubles we had been outliers, but now I was better trained, more experienced, and rowing in an appropriate class — though the Senior Masters Single was still a tough, demanding event. To finish in the normal range would certify me as a genuine member of the rowing community. Once and for all, I wanted to prove that, yes, I *could* play with the big boys.

In the rowing world I still felt like an outsider, a journalist, an observer. I was a hack rower with his face pressed against the window, enjoying an excellent view of the party — and so close to it! — but I had not earned the right to come inside. In fact, the door was unlatched; I had simply been unwilling to walk in. I declined to call myself a bona fide oarsman, in part because I lacked the classic rowing credentials, never having been on a school or college crew (I didn't count my months as a freshman cox), much less a national team. I was an autodidact, unauthorized to accredit myself.

My rowing peers, in contrast, did not seem to doubt my status and sometimes hailed milestones in my progress. One day I rowed a competitive workout with a few single scullers from Weld Boat Club, whose boathouse is a mile downstream from my club. When I returned to our dock, I was greeted by one of the more experienced oarsmen, Ed Jans. I told Ed that I had rowed well and even had the satisfaction of passing a couple of boats. "Ah, you've drawn blood," he announced, smiling broadly. "If you were a *Mafioso*, they'd say, 'You've made your bones.'"

The Head training brought strict organization to my rowing workouts. Joe Bouscaren, a onetime world-class sculler who was still in superb competitive form, gave me a basic workout regime. Monday was an "easy" day — four fifteen-minute pieces at very low ratings. At low ratings — and consequent slow speeds — the boat is much less stable, so this workout immersed me in the discipline of setting up the shell, which tends to wobble fearfully on the recovery when the strokes come so far apart. In each piece I rowed four minutes at 16 strokes per minute, then three minutes at 18, two minutes at 20, and one minute at 22, then tapered down with two minutes at 20 and three at 18 for a total of fifteen minutes in all. Rest two minutes by paddling along gently. Then three more of the same fifteen-minute pieces. That was the easy day.

Tuesdays were a "medium" day, calling for four to six ten-minute pieces rowed at medium-hard pressure, ratings from 24 to 30. This workout aims to achieve a level of intensity called the anaerobic threshold (AT), namely, the maximal exertion that aerobic metabolism allows; anything more strenuous would push the body into the anaerobic zone. These pieces began with four minutes at

24, then three minutes at 26, two at 28, and a final minute at 30. The AT workouts expand endurance, the ability to work hard for extended periods.

Wednesday was a "hard" day, prescribing five five-minute pieces rowed at full pressure, and as for stroke rating, Joe told me, "the sky's the limit." In my case the sky was not much higher than 30, but full pressure for five minutes at 30 was quite sufficient to get me sucking air into my lungs by any possible means; it was a devastatingly taxing piece to complete. Like interval training, the hard workouts raise the high end of our capacity for intense exertion. To finish five of these was to me an amazing feat; at the end of the workout I would sometimes ask myself, Did I really do that?

Thursday, Friday, and Saturday repeated the same easy-medium-hard progression, and on Sunday, citing divine precedent, I rested.

Training was exhausting. Although I had been rowing six days a week for several months, this was a whole new level of effort. In the boathouse's logbook, my entries jumped from four to five miles a day to six to ten miles daily. I was no longer rowing a particular route (hence a certain distance) on the river; now my task was to complete my daily program, which was carrying me over much greater mileage.

It was also important to row as efficiently as possible. So I sought out private coaching to improve my technique. I worked with Dan Boyne, who runs the sculling program at Harvard, and Holly Metcalf, a 1984 Olympic gold medalist who has coached in Boston for many years. I paid these mentors an hourly rate to take a motor launch out, observe my sculling, and coach me one-on-one. They had much to do. During my first hour with Holly, she had me drop and relax my shoulders and apply my lower body much more to the leg drive. By the end of that hour I was rowing a new stroke: I could reach out farther at the catch, and I felt stronger when the oars were in the water, since I was loading bigger muscle groups onto the blades. "It's strange, Holly," I told her, "but I actually feel like a bigger guy." She smiled back at me. "Well, you know what? You *look* like a bigger guy now," she said, "because you're a lot longer through the water."

There is being big, and then there is rowing big. Physical size, which I had always viewed as an absolute, immutable factor — and one that rarely worked in my favor — turned out to be a relative matter. There was tape-measured size, and then there was effective size. Dan Boyne, who studied martial arts, observed that there were some big athletes who "fought small." They didn't use their size in combat: for example, they might not fully extend their arms to deliver blows or kick out completely with their legs. They confined themselves to a smaller orbit of motion, fighting inside an invisible box. That box was made of self-concepts: "fighting small" is a stunted form of self-expression. These boxed-in athletes had no advantage over smaller opponents who "fought big."

In rowing the same thing happens. Larry Klecatsky, a 5-foot 9-inch 145-pound oarsman, is arguably the greatest single sculler the United States has ever produced. He has won more national championships (sixty-four) than any other rower. As a lightweight, he made the 1976 Olympic team and rowed in the heavyweight double at Montreal. Until he was fifty years old, Klecatsky rowed competitively in *open* events, and he is still a dominant force at the Head of the Charles Regatta, which he has won more times than any other single sculler. Using a marvelously long reach, Klecatsky rows big, and wins.

Sculling, done well, is an easy, frictionless motion that brings the boat and rower together as one. We are not hauling the boat upstream so much as coaxing it forward. As we stop struggling against physical laws, we remove conflict from our stroke and speed becomes a simpler matter. We no longer work to overcome inertia — a body at rest tends to remain at rest — but we use it: a body in motion tends to remain in motion. Doing less, we go faster. So much òf success in sports comes from having a quiet body — one that makes no unnecessary moves. Steve Fairbairn, a famous coach at Jesus College, Cambridge, had a simple axiom: "If you can't do it easily," he said, "you can't do it at all."

We feel things with the whole body — not only the skin, but virtually all our cells. However, the sense organs for sight, hearing, taste, and smell reside in the upper part of the body, specifically the head. Most of our expressive acts also originate in the upper body: voice, facial expression, posture, gestures. If the upper body fosters communication and contact, the lower half supports us and generates power. Our largest muscle groups are below the waist. Consequently all forms of aerobic exercise involve moving the legs, stirring a demand for oxygen from big muscles like the quadriceps and gluteus maximus.

The lower body is the source of power in sports. In rowing, the leg drive is the main propulsive force on the oars. Although the arms pull the oar in to the body to complete the stroke, their main function is simply to connect the rower, like a pair of cables, to the oar handles. Keeping the upper body still provides a fixed horizon, a base of sensory perception that permits the accurate and effective application of power. For example, a golfer with a quiet upper body can keep a steady sight line on the ball while uncoiling the power of the swing from the legs and hips, as released through the arms. Swinging a tennis or squash racquet, baseball bat, or lacrosse stick involves the same kinetic chain.

The electronic engineers' concept of signal-to-noise ratio describes the clarity of a communications channel. Signal is the pure message content of a communication — a sentence spoken into a telephone, a picture transmitted to a television receiver, a bar of music broadcast on a radio station. Noise, on the other hand, refers to random inputs in the channel — crosstalk on the phone connection, "snow" on the television screen, static on the radio station. Noise amounts to random wavelengths that interfere with the reception of the desired wavelength. The higher the ratio of signal to noise, the more easily and clearly a message can be communicated. A high signal-to-noise ratio means clear sound and sharp pictures.

Every act of communication involves a signal-to-noise ratio. The key factor is *ratio:* it is a matter of foreground-background. Many of us try to strengthen our communications by increasing the signal. But as media multiply and levels of signal rise higher and higher, modern society has become an unrelieved shouting match. To get attention and have one's message clearly received, the essential is not more signal, but less noise. Communication means creating a quiet channel in which the desired signal will appear and so produce a high ratio of signal to noise. We do not need more input, but less distraction. *Suppress noise.*

In sports the same rule applies. To gain greater effect as athletes, we do not necessarily have to do more. The secret may be to do *less,* to suppress noise. When hitting a golf ball, tennis ball, or baseball, we still the upper body. *Keep the head down.* The same applies to a corner kick in soccer or a field goal in football. The skilled athlete eliminates motions that do not serve the desired result. Our tomato plants thrive when we weed the garden.

One morning, Dan Boyne demonstrated what coaches are paid to do: he pointed out something obvious that I never would have noticed on my own. "Make sure you finish every stroke with your hands at the same height," Dan said. "You're varying the finish quite a bit." I began keeping my finish uniform, and suddenly the shell set up like a rock. My inconsistent finishes had been wagging the boat all over the place. Similarly, Holly simplified my rowing stroke by quieting my upper body — keeping my head, shoulders, arms, and torso still, as a fixed fulcrum for the oars rather than a noisy group of inputs that was corrupting my set.

Successful rowing grows from consistency: uniform causes produce uniform effects. If we wish to keep a boat level and move it at a steady — preferably a high — velocity, then identical strokes — same oar height, length, pressure, and rate — are desirable. All these factors can vary, but preferably at our choice: they do not change randomly but intentionally. This can only happen if we have brought each of these factors under conscious control. One way to do this is through uniformity. If we can teach ourselves to row each stroke at exactly the same length, we will gradually master length, and then we can vary it at will.

Lawrence "Monk" Terry, Jr., who stroked the U.S. eight that won a silver medal at the 1972 Olympics, had such consistency. "With Monk, the last stroke of the race was exactly the same as the first one," said Fritz Hobbs, one of his crewmates. That is very high praise. When we can replicate a particular result at will — be it a long, balanced sculling stroke, a topspin forehand, or a perfect mocha soufflé, we become confident in that activity. It is ours.

Consistency and uniformity have been key elements in the McDonald's fast-food empire, and in the fast-food industry as a whole. McDonald's built its image on replication: every McDonald's outlet, everywhere in the world, offers the same basic menu of fast food, the same golden arches and the same standard of cleanliness, the same entry-level workers in the same uniforms dispensing the same french fries. Repeating this imagery over and over again established a known, reliable identity for the chain. Pounding away relentlessly on such core themes is a marketing strategy known as "slugging the public."

Or consider replication in music. The improvisations of the jazz saxophonist John Coltrane displayed immense agility. Coltrane's solos often included astonishing bursts of a dazzling number of notes in a few bars. Yet in his own practice sessions, Coltrane sometimes ignored runs; what he did play consistently was long tones, whole notes. By gaining full command of each individual note, he could later combine many notes without sacrificing tone quality. Having mastered the tone, he could then play with its duration and sequencing.

Under Harry Parker, Harvard crews have buried opponents with consistency. Of course the athletes are superbly trained; they work hard all year long and accomplish a great deal in the daily ninety-minute sessions that Parker runs so efficiently. At the starting line, the Harvard boats know they are at least as well prepared as any opponent.

Furthermore, they have not only trained, but competed as they trained. Newell Boathouse is a competition laboratory. In workouts, the Harvard boats race each other, and individuals vie for both seats in the varsity boat and simple supremacy. Race day is nothing new: the oarsmen of Newell have been racing every day.

Perhaps because of Harvard's awesome history (Parker's track record from 1963 to 1998 is 134–31, an .812 winning percentage), opposing crews often like to seize the lead early, perhaps hoping for psychological intimidation. They have rarely if ever accomplished any such thing. Trailing at the start is nothing new to Harvard oarsmen; they have come from behind for most of three decades. Typically, they will be going fast enough so that any opponents ahead of them must be failing to pace themselves and hence are going *too fast.* Grabbing that early lead costs energy, an expense that may later haunt the front-runner. This is especially true in long races like the four-miler that Harvard and Yale row each June. In such a contest, which takes around twenty minutes to row, it is quite possible to be two or three boat lengths ahead early in the race and still lose badly. In practice, Parker would remind his rowers that when opponents jump out in front, you must *make them pay the price.*

Since crew is an endurance sport that makes such encompassing demands on the body and requires a big anaerobic push at the start to get the shell up to racing speed, it does tend to build lactic acid in the muscles, which causes sustained discomfort. This is one reason that carefully pacing oneself is essential.

However, too much has been made of pain in rowing. The rowing community has perhaps bought into our society's worship of suffering, our readiness to find moral virtue in the ability to endure pain. Yet, competitively, there is no virtue in pain. In the middle of a race, you want your crew to be rowing powerfully but comfortably, taking good deep lungfuls of air, striking the water in a cadence that feels natural, rowing with composure at a controlled pace. The hellish images of pain — the scorched lungs, the sands of the Sahara inching through one's blood vessels — are what you want the other crew to be feeling. Let *them* row on the river Styx, make *them* pay the price.

Regattas are won incrementally, one stroke at a time. Victory results from the accumulation of small effects, like dripping water wearing a groove in a rock, drop by drop. Consider, for the sake of argument, that it takes an eight-oared crew 200 strokes (a low but round number) to cover a 2,000-meter racecourse. In this case each stroke advances the boat 10 meters, about 33 feet. Now suppose we row just slightly better — one-half of 1 percent better — than our opponents. On each stroke we travel 5 centimeters (about 2 inches) farther than they do. If both crews row the race at identical stroke rates, after 200 strokes we will be 10 meters ahead, winning by half a boat length *on a 2-inch advantage.* If we row *1* percent better — 4 inches per stroke — we win by a full length, around 60 feet.

Thus do the visible effects of the invisible manifest themselves. A spectator at the regatta would not see that 2-inch advantage on each stroke but will certainly see the half-length margin at the finish line. Success results from a relentless accumulation of small effects that grow into a critical mass that becomes invincible.

Many years after college, one Harvard oarsman joined a large Boston bank that was facing a difficult task. The bank had many loans secured by real estate that had plunged in value after the 1987 stock market crash. The loans were going into default, and the banker's job was to sit down with each of the customers and insist that they repay the bank. For some of these debtors, meeting their obligation meant enormous sacrifices — liquidating retirement savings, selling their houses, radically lowering their families' standard of living. Yet the former rower had to talk with each of these customers face to face and virtually pound his fist on the table and demand repayment of the loans.

Although the bank was simply asking for its due, it was a classic banker-as-villain setup, an unpleasant situation. Furthermore, there were so many loans in default that the executive knew that these unpleasant scenarios would dominate his days for the next three years. "There was only one way I was able to get through it," he said. "I approached this job the same way you row the four-miler against Yale. If you think about how far you have to go and how much pain you are going to feel, you've had it. The only way to get through it is one stroke at a time."

Winning by the accumulation of small effects works miracles. However, victory by increments has slipped in popularity. We have become an infantile society that expects immediate gratification, as in the "instant win" lottery ticket. Citizens buy gambling tickets in the hope that, without producing anything or exercising any faculty, they will immediately become multimillionaires. Students graduate from college with plans to sell their first screenplay for half a million dollars. We are losing our patience; as a culture, we are becoming disinclined to earn our rewards. Obsessed with results and winning, we downplay the journey in favor of the destination; if we could, we might omit the trip entirely. A winning lottery ticket is an arrival without a journey.

We may be starting to resemble the laboratory rats who were offered two buttons to push. One released a food pellet, the other electrically stimulated a pleasure center in the brain. Many rats did nothing but tickle their pleasure centers until they died — of starvation. They ignored real nutrition in favor of instant gratification, preferring the result without the process. Similarly, recreational drugs offer a chemical shortcut to pleasure, avoiding those real-world transactions that produce harder won, yet more lasting, results.

Rowing, however, sets the clock back a century to the Horatio Alger era of earning one's success. No market forces offer incentives to excel in crew. We do it for the mystery and joy of the process, which proceeds by tiny, nearly imperceptible increments. At first the distinctions are so small that only those of us in the boats can recognize them. But at the finish line they are evident to the world. *Attention to trifles is what makes for perfection,* said Michelangelo, *and perfection is no trifle.*

In the Head of the Charles, the perfection I sought was simply rowing my best. As I rowed more Head pieces and watched my times over the course steadily improve, I came to believe that if no disasters befell me and I sculled to my potential, I might well earn my spot on the normal curve. I wouldn't know this for certain until after the race, since the field of competitors actually "draws" that normal curve as it races up the river. Who knew how fast they — we — might be?

◆

Ultimately we train for life. We build training into our lives; it becomes part of our routine. Training is not something added as a temporary intervention or a "fix-it" maneuver for some special event. We will be in training forever. The payoffs, too, are endless; energy and discipline, which training creates, are key factors in any endeavor.

The human body loves routine: physically, we function best within patterns. During the rowing season I rise daily at 5:30 A.M., meditate for twenty minutes, have a cup of English Breakfast tea, and arrive at the boathouse by 6:30 A.M. At the start of the season, if I set my alarm clock and enforce this routine for four consecutive days, by the fifth day I will awaken naturally at 5:30 and magically find myself at the dock an hour later.

With discipline we can program ourselves with new routines. If — and only if — we are consistent in our practice, these routines will become habits, freeing us to focus the tool of discipline on conquering new territories. Consistency is vital; if our behavior is erratic, we send mixed signals to the brain and nervous system, giving them no clear pattern to follow. Therefore "exceptions" can be fatal to progress, at least until the new habit is firmly in place.

Even when training has become a lifelong practice, it can be helpful to train for a race. A specific personal goal backlights many life decisions. During the months before the Head, as my mileage increased and I minimized dietary fat, I lost fifteen pounds. Choices about how to spend my time, how long to sleep and when to rise, what to eat, which conversations to have, whether to enter other races, how to spend money, all contributed to — or compromised — my racing goal. It can be refreshing to live this way for a few months, and competitive rowers may do so for years, even decades. Things fall into place around the number-one priority.

I began rowing timed Head pieces — yes, and double Head pieces — with Gordon Hamilton's group of Cambridge Boat Club scullers on Tuesdays. On Thursdays, I sculled from Weld Boathouse with Dan Boyne and a different group of Head entrants. And on Saturday mornings, starting a few weeks before the race, anyone who desired the experience was welcome to meet at the starting line and row a Head piece with about forty to fifty other single scullers, including some very fast company. All these experiences taught me to race and to navigate through traffic. The group Head pieces are dry runs, rowed by highly competitive, intense athletes who are hell-bent on getting up the course as quickly as possible. They are quick to chastise anyone who seems to be obstructing their way. In all these training groups, we *raced*. It is a rough-and-tumble way to train, and it is highly effective. *I never practice*, said the harpsichordist Wanda Landowska, *I only play*.

At the Saturday morning Head pieces, we start in approximate reverse order of speed, so, as with all my training flotillas, I am among the first to go off. Today I start a few seconds ahead of one of the more dedicated men in my club. Mark has been training hard; I have seen him on the dock nearly every morning. He and I are about equal in speed. Early in the race, I outsteer Mark around a couple of river bends and increase my lead, but at the powerhouse stretch I keep a steady pace while he pushes harder, and he closes to about twenty meters. I see him moving up: you know you are losing ground in a regatta when the boats behind you get bigger. Mark's push toward me triggers a Stone Age reaction: *I'll be damned if I'm going to let him catch me.*

And so the battle is on. Mark relentlessly maintains his pace; he keeps coming at me. Every few strokes he looks over his shoulder, to steer and to check his position. We fight these naval battles with oars, muscles, and minds: if Mark notices he is gaining on me, that will encourage him. He will think: it's only a matter of time. Hence I will not let myself be reeled in. I concentrate on long strokes, rhythm, keeping the run of the boat strong.

Leading in a boat race can feel like being chased by a predator: to be caught would mean death. This morning, on this river, I am the prey, and thousands of years of survival instincts metabolize fear into boat speed. It is more than competition, it is self-preservation, outrunning an assailant. This is both an edge and a disadvantage. As the lead boat, facing astern, I can see who is behind me, who is coming up, and at what speed. But Mark often does not know where he stands. This is the advantage of being behind: you focus on your own rowing, undistracted by worries about the competition. Hence you row better, perhaps even well enough to catch the leader. Knowing this, savvy coxswains sometimes feed their crews little information about where they stand in the race.

In an eight, it is thrilling to catch another boat after trailing by a long distance. As you get closer you begin hearing their coxswain, at first muffled, then with increasing clarity as the gap narrows. *We can make out the cox's words; we are reeling them in.* Drawing even to and then passing the other shell — "rowing through them" — is charged with polarities: abysmally deflating for the boat being passed, a prolonged crescendo of triumph for the overtaking crew.

But not today. Mark will enjoy no such moment in this Head piece. For the last two miles I hold off his charge, keeping him in his place, frustrating his bumptious efforts to catch me. It must be terribly demoralizing to keep rowing so hard for so long and still make not a foot's progress against my wake. Perhaps he hopes that my endurance will give out and he will get past me in the final stretch. Not so. My stamina holds up, and in fact, over the last half mile I open up another boat length of open water. Perhaps it was *his* endurance that gave out, or maybe he folded psychologically on realizing he was not going to catch me.

At the finish line I check my stopwatch and see that I have set another personal best for the Head course. I have Mark to thank, for impelling me onward. Ultimately, in a head race we are not competing against each other but against the clock and against our own benchmarks. Yet in a race with other people, a human race, the predatory chase always carries a whiff of mortality. For a fleeting moment, before we again avert our eyes, we recognize that the stopwatch is not the clock we are really racing against.

The Charles River's serpentine course enhances the role of steering. For decades scullers have debated how to cut each turn, where a boat should be on each stretch of the river to steer an optimal route. There is consensus on the main points, and anyone who belongs to the Boston rowing tribe can learn how to navigate a good Head course.

But I had an edge: my friend Tom Tiffany is one of the most experienced coxswains anywhere, and he has an especially good feel for the course, having raced it since the 1960s. One day Tom followed me in a motor launch as I rowed a Head piece. At crucial places he explained where — and why — to start turns and recommended good steering points. Thus I was able to refine the "basic" Head course and groove its contours into memory over the following weeks.

Steering well is the best revenge. It's a crucial weapon, especially for smaller athletes: we may not be able to overpower the opposition, but we can outsteer them, and on this river that can mean a lot. In the Head, a cox like Tiffany could cut ten seconds or more from an eight's time. Listening to him might produce similar results for me.

Yet training workouts, rowed in isolation, are a fool's paradise. On race day, other boats may prevent us from taking that ideal route we have traced in our minds. The group dry runs therefore add a crucial element: traffic. We cannot test our models only in the lab, but must eventually expose them to the capricious world of reality.

Laboratories strictly control experimental conditions, attempting to weed out confounding variables. Yet the crisp restrictions, like solo workouts, paint a false picture. Outdoors, in the world of raw, unmanaged experience, controlled conditions rarely, if ever, arise. In one way or another, chance influences every ongoing process and so erodes the purity of the scientific laws established in sterile environments.

Upstream from Eliot Bridge, I see him coming through the arch, heading toward me, and this guy is *cranking*. His back seems to enlarge every couple of strokes, and anybody who closes at that rate is moving fast. Personally, I am in no hurry. I'm dawdling along, only a couple of minutes into my warm-up, so I decide to enjoy watching this thunderbolt approach.

The white hull approaching me is a Van Dusen, one of the world's high-end racing shells. Yet the oars are wooden — a throwback to twenty or thirty years ago. About 98 percent of rowers now use some variant of carbon-fiber oars. To see wooden oars on a Van Dusen is like seeing someone with an oversize graphite tennis racquet wearing canvas tennis shoes from the 1960s.

No matter. Whatever this guy is doing is working. The back of his shirt reads, N.Y.A.C. — New York Athletic Club, in Pelham Bay, New York, the home of several world-class scullers. He could be one of them. But rowing shirts do not reliably indicate their wearers' roots: shirts are won in bets, traded, sold, bartered; they circulate around the world. My own collection includes shirts from Bulgaria, New Zealand, and the former Soviet Union, places I have never seen. As he draws near, I recognize that this fierce sculler is not from N.Y.A.C. In fact, his boathouse is only a mile downstream. The Olympian overtaking me is Harry Parker, who smiles fleetingly, or perhaps winces, as he goes by, pulling too hard to do more. Being Harry, he might have done the same even on a light paddle.

Harry was pushing himself. Sessions like this — solo workouts in the single — are perhaps the ultimate test of self-determination. In a race, pushing yourself hard is a given; the hormonal excitement of competition elicits maximal efforts: witness my own personal bests at CRASH-B and fending off Mark's charge up the Head course. With a coach present we do not slack off, since we have an unusually attentive spectator. Rowing in a crew applies group pressure to meet the crew's standards, which we hope are high ones — if not, it's time to find another crew.

But practicing in a single we answer only to ourselves: we are coach, crew, and competition. Only our inner drives can offset the body's natural resistance to hard, stressful work. Structured workouts, like the easy-medium-hard sequence I undertook, help: timed pieces and prescribed stroke ratings provide a baseline of accountability. But there remains the imponderable question of *pressure:* how hard do you pull?

Rowers have several vague terms to describe pressure, ranging from hardest to lightest: full pressure, three-quarters pressure, half pressure, paddle. In a race, a cox may call a "power ten" or "power twenty," indicating that for the next ten or twenty strokes, the crew is really going to hit it, giving it everything they have. Paradoxically, this suggests that there is a level of effort beyond full pressure, since in a race, we are supposedly already rowing at full pressure all the way down the course.

How full is full? It depends in part on how long the piece lasts. If a coach asks me to row five strokes at full pressure, I can go savage, throwing myself all-out into those five strokes, which will indeed be impressive ones. Yet I could never row the three miles of the Head of the Charles — roughly 600 strokes — at that intensity. I would quickly burn myself out and end up rowing the largest part of the race at considerably less than full pressure, as defined by my usual standards.

In long pieces we must pace ourselves, but in a workout we must also push ourselves. We must test how completely we can inhabit the meaning of "full pressure." What we bring to the starting line on race day depends on how far we have stretched our capacities in practice.

Suppose you own a fine restaurant and face a problem: your head chef will soon depart for a job in another city. Your customers not only expect an elegant setting, attentive service, and superb food but want to be surprised by the kitchen's creativity. In this high-end market it will not do to serve the same wild mushroom risotto that is available elsewhere.

Culinary creativity, like full pressure in rowing, has no exact definition. It means pushing oneself to a personal horizon, defined only by our own standards. Running a kitchen that can get out eighty plates for dinner in a timely manner is one thing, but developing new combinations of flavors, textures, scents, and presentations on those plates is another. Creativity in the kitchen grows from the chef's talent, training, experience, and passion for invention. And, like full pressure on the oar, a demanding competitive environment — as well as high aspirations — can help to sustain this quality.

In my single I established a discipline: to row my solo workouts as if a coach were present. I did not always succeed in this, but remembering that principle took me in the right direction. A Zen proverb advises, *When alone act as you would with company; when receiving guests, maintain the same demeanor as when alone.* The point is not to ignore the social context but to maintain integrity: at all times be true to yourself.

It is important to keep one's own counsel because rowers hear so much diverse opinion — from coaches, books, magazines, fellow rowers — about how to row effectively. On any given morning on any dock, there will be three or four different ideas available concerning how far to lay back at the release or when to start swinging the back during the drive. Over the years, I have been exposed to enough contradictory advice to confuse a Zen master. If I tried to put into practice everything I've been told, I would look like a lunatic in the boat, with different parts of my body working at cross purposes.

Yet confusion arises only when we try to make sense of all this data in our minds. Most of the advice is indeed valid, but very little of it is universally applicable. All the coaching I've received has not befuddled me because I have tested these precepts physically, in the boat. The body has a senior wisdom that tells us what advice works *for us* and what is merely "good advice" we should throw overboard.

Jack Barnaby, Harvard's tennis and squash coach from 1937 to 1976, compiled an amazing record. To single out one especially fertile period, from 1961 to 1973 his teams went 120–3, winning eleven intercollegiate championships. People often asked what Barnaby's "system" was, and his answer was, "To avoid all systems like the plague. Adapt to the individual."

One could watch the nine players on Jack's varsity and never imagine that they had the same coach, their styles were so diverse. If someone was a big, hard-hitting player, Jack would amplify that strength and make him into a real hitter who could overpower opponents. In contrast, if an athlete had a deft touch and a risk-taking temperament, Jack coached him as a shot-maker who could win with finesse. A player who was incredibly quick would learn to volley everything in sight and wear opponents out with pace. Jack built winning games around the native strengths of each individual rather than teaching any ideal way to play squash.

He believed in sound technique and taught it relentlessly, but Jack also kept technical matters in perspective. In recent decades we have been losing that perspective, and not only in sports. Our society has begun to worship technique. We seek formulas for success. In every sport, art, and profession, even in our personal lives, we consult books, tapes, seminars, and classes that aim to inculcate the proper technique for doing almost anything, from hitting a seven-iron to managing a sales force to having sex. The glut of advice begins to persuade us that there is a correct way to do everything. Technical advice has become a Procrustean bed.

Yet the creators who have changed this world have not done so by applying a formula, no matter if it comes from Ted Williams, Martha Graham, or Lee Strasberg. To create we must *crash the system*. In sports, the great champions have reshaped their sport in their own image, breaking all the rules and received wisdom that stood in their way.

For example, in bowling, one technical universal is that a right-handed bowler must release the ball with the weight on the left foot; conversely, a lefty bowls "off" the right foot. This makes eminent sense for several technical reasons, like maintaining balance and not hitting one's ankle with the bowling ball as it is rolled. But in the 1950s, a right-handed bowler named Lou Campi, nicknamed "Wrong-Foot Louie," bowled off his right foot. Campi had played bocce before taking up bowling and had learned a style of rolling balls that felt natural to him. His technique was dead wrong, but it worked for him. Despite the technical heresy, Campi became one of the top professional bowlers in the United States.

In tennis in the 1960s, the received wisdom was that any two-handed backhand was fatally flawed: it would shorten one's reach. Then Jimmy Connors came along in the 1970s and, with great quickness and anticipation, covered the court so well that he neutralized that objection. His two-handed backhand became one of the great offensive weapons in the game.

Crash the system. Champions win by finding out who they are and then building a winning game on their unique mental and physical aptitudes. In rowing, Anne Marden's sculling technique defied several well-established principles. She brought her arms into the stroke too early and finished roughly, laying back exceptionally far toward the bow. Yet she was the fastest woman sculler in the United States for several years and won a silver medal at the 1988 Seoul Olympics. Some coaches shook their heads when Marden rowed by, muttering that with proper technique she could go even faster. Perhaps so, but "proper technique" might also have slowed her down.

Whether it be T. S. Eliot, Julia Child, or Michael Jordan, creators express their individuality in their chosen medium. In one way or another, they sign their work. Innovators do absorb tradition and technique, but these become the servants of their individual genius. What they produce reshapes their medium in a way that places their personal vision above and beyond any formula.

Over the last third of a century, Harry Parker has stayed on the leading edge of the sport of rowing, each year devising fresh mixtures of tradition and the individual talent. An innovator from the start, Harry was among the first to introduce year-round conditioning and to use the ergometer for both evaluation and training of athletes. In the 1960s his crews rowed in advanced Stämpfli shells from Switzerland and successfully experimented with so-called German or tandem riggings, which put, for example, both the #4 and #5 oars on the starboard side of the boat. His athletes trained by running up and down sections of Harvard's football stadium, building endurance and the iron-hard quadriceps that power the leg drive, the wellspring of energy in the rowing stroke.

Harry runs stadiums alongside his crew. One way that he has stayed in excellent physical condition has been by training with the athletes; every year, in effect, Harry Parker himself goes out for the

Harvard crew. This is no casual undertaking. Running stadiums makes a StairMaster workout feel about as demanding as a nap. The first time I tried it, I walked rather than ran the tiers, and even so, I was perspiring and breathing hard after only two sections of the thirty-seven in the stadium. In Harvard crew parlance, to complete a circuit of all thirty-seven sections is to make a *tour de stade*. Even more exhausting is the "century" — up and down a hundred sections. Harry once ran a century with one of the all-time great stadium runners, Charlie Altekruse; sprinting toward the end, Parker finished in 59:50, making his goal of a century in under an hour. This represents a blistering pace of 36 seconds per section, but the astounding thing is having the physical and mental discipline to maintain that pace for a hundred sections.

Parker leads by example, not exhortation. His deeds corroborate (and, some say, outnumber) his words. Harry does not give dramatic speeches about winning one for Harvard. The finishing sprint is not about doing it for something or somebody else; that is too thin a reed to sustain such exploits. Strong bonds do form among the Harvard oarsmen, and these relationships surely expand their horizons: each man doesn't want to let his teammates down. Yet Parker understands that willfulness ultimately comes from within: we don't want to let *ourselves* down, to stop short of our own potential.

There have been junior varsity oarsmen who might have made the varsity if Parker had given them a kick in the pants. Harry never bothered. A rower who was not pushing himself for his own reasons had already disqualified himself from the varsity. If willfulness needs any external support, we must wonder if it might not collapse at the critical moment, when the going gets very tough indeed and the oarsman can ask only himself whether *he* will take No for an answer.

◆

When all members of a crew are willing to launch themselves into the unknown, a collective magic arises. In the eight-oared finals of the 1936 Olympics, the University of Washington varsity conjured up this magic to disappoint an immense crowd of Germans, whose own crew was reportedly "galvanized into action at the sight of Hitler on the boathouse balcony." Fighting a fierce crosswind, the Americans were in fifth place at the halfway mark, but approaching the finish they had closed to battle Italy and Germany for the gold medal as the partisan crowd chanted, *"Deutsch-land! Deutschland!"* in time with the German stroke. But the Americans, rowing to a different drummer, came through the two Axis eights and won the gold medal. George Pocock, who built Washington's boat and witnessed that race, later wrote:

> To be of championship caliber, a crew must have total confidence in each other, able to drive with abandon, confident that no man will get the full weight of the pull. Without this confidence, the men tend to "row with the boat," meaning they will not pull faster than the boat is going. A good run between strokes is impossible under these conditions because the oarsmen have to rush up on the slide for the next stroke to attain a higher beat. The 1936 crew, with Hume at stroke, rowed with abandon, beautifully timed. Having complete confidence in one another, they would bound on the stroke with one powerful cut; then ghost forward to the next stroke with the boat running true and with hardly a perceptible slow-down.

The will to excel resides within each individual. No coach can install it; the impulse to explore one's full potential flows from inner wellsprings or not at all. "Motivational" exhortation cannot invent willfulness.

This suggests a Taoist code of management. "The best way to

manage anything is by making use of its own nature," says the *Tao Te Ching.* "The world is ruled by letting things take their course. It cannot be ruled by interfering." To build a winning crew, select the right athletes, place them in the proper seats, and allow them the freedom to create. In other words, hire the right people for the right jobs and manage with a long, loose leash.

Harry Parker may not be a Taoist, but neither is he a motivational speaker. Parker is a man of few words. By not giving his rowers too many instructions, he empowers them, trusting them to discover how to perfect their own oarsmanship. Harry watches workouts closely and is enormously present during practices, but says little. When he speaks, however, the oarsmen attend to his every word. *Those who know do not say; those who say do not know.* "He never told us we were good enough," recalled one rower. "So we would work harder to resolve an uncertainty."

Jake Fiechter was one of the few oarsmen who rowed for both Harry Parker and Ted Nash, who not only coached at the University of Pennsylvania but also coached many elite rowers, and has been a member of every U.S. Olympic team since 1960, as either a rower or a coach. In 1968, a year after graduating from Harvard, Jake tried out for the U.S. Olympic team in the pair, coached by Ted Nash. Unlike Harry, Ted is a talkative, heart-on-his-sleeve personality who dishes out ample doses of motivational support. At the 1968 Olympic trials, as Fiechter was about to get into his boat at the dock, he saw a piece of tape that Nash had placed on his foot stretchers. On it was a single word: PRIDE.

No such thing would ever appear in a boat launching from Newell Boathouse. There, the philosophy is a Darwinian one of the cream rising to the top. Motivation is assumed. This assumption works at Harvard, whose students are a highly achievement-oriented, competitive slice of humanity. Such overachievers might be seeking validation, winning outer superiority to assuage inner feelings of inadequacy. I myself at times have surely sought the world's approval in order to justify approval of myself. Even so, I have generally aimed for my own targets rather than any external ones.

"You developed a much greater degree of self-confidence rowing for Harry," says Tiff Wood. "You knew that *you* were doing it — it was *your* desire to win, not Harry's." One Harvard coxswain, Paul Hoffman, explains that "you had to be doing this for yourself, and once you reached that conclusion, the standard never had a top end, since you were always working against the horizon." When an athlete strives to satisfy a coach's expectations, those expectations become a limiting factor. There is no space to pour one's passion if the coach is in the spotlight. But Parker, the accidental Taoist, gets out of the way. There is no top end.

The result of this infinite horizon is that Harvard crews sometimes seem to accomplish miracles, outcomes that theoretically should not happen. The creative power of consciousness overrides the objections of the material world.

Consider the 1979 Harvard-Yale race, one of the greatest crew races of all time. That year, Harvard was the underdog in the four-miler even though they had won the San Diego Crew Classic that April and had been undefeated going into the Eastern Sprints in May. But Yale, with a big, powerful crew stroked by future Olympian John Biglow, also entered the Sprints undefeated, and rowing into a strong headwind, beat Harvard there by a full length. Hence Yale's crew established themselves as the favorites in the June four-miler, a race more than triple the length of the 2,000-meter Sprints distance.

Yale's monster crew outweighed Harvard by an average of fifteen to twenty pounds per man. Yet at Red Top, the camp on the Thames River in New London, Connecticut, where Harvard trains for the Yale race, the oarsmen radiated willfulness. *It doesn't matter if they're a better crew, they have to row a better race.*

Race day was dead calm, a boost for the smaller crew, since bigger oarsmen have an advantage in muscling through a headwind. Here is what happened, as described by Harry Parker:

In the four-mile race, Yale took advantage of its superior size and power and drew out to an immediate lead of one length, rowing at an aggressive 36 strokes per minute. They seemed determined to discourage the smaller Harvard crew early in the race. But Harvard, led by stroke Gordie Gardiner and rowing at 34 strokes per minute, held on tenaciously and limited Yale to that one-length lead. At every half-mile flag, Biglow threw in an aggressive, powerful "power ten" and Yale would ease out another seat or two. Gardiner, rowing a very controlled 34, would respond and Harvard would pull back to within one length. The same sequence occurred at 1 mile, 1½ miles, and 2 miles. Finally, at the 2½-mile mark, Harvard's power ten moved them back within ¾ of a length. Biglow, still stroking at a punishing 36 strokes per minute, saw this and immediately drove harder to keep Harvard behind him. At three miles gone, he took another burst, stubbornly resisting the Harvard charge. But Harvard, sensing momentum swinging its way, drove even harder and began to draw even.

With ¾ of a mile to go, and just as Harvard was about to draw even, Biglow squeezed another burst from his crew and retook the lead. Gardiner responded immediately and drove Harvard into the lead at the final half-mile flag; he pushed his crew at a furious pace to a half-length lead. Biglow, however, despite being passed late in such an exhausting race, was still not finished and drove his crew once again to close the margin slightly in the last ¼ mile. Harvard finished ⅓ of a length ahead and both crews were well under the previous record for an "upstream" race. The race was a magnificent duel between the two best crews in the country, led by two extremely savvy and aggressive strokes.

Theoretically, there is no way Harvard should have won that race. But they used all their weapons — training, fitness, patience, will — and prevailed, rebuking the calculations of the material world. A Radcliffe coach who watched the race said, "I've never seen a braver effort by a crew. I was in tears, it was such a moving experience."

If you examine Harvard's record over the last few decades, the thing you'll find missing is the big loss — the crucial race where its crew came up a bit short. It doesn't happen that way; it's the other crew that comes up short. For example, at the 1968 Olympic trials in Long Beach, California, Harvard had a showdown with Penn, having beaten the Quakers twice that spring. Parker was facing his mentor Joe Burk, who was one year away from retirement. After 1,500 meters of the 2,000-meter race, Penn was nearly half a length ahead. But then began the Harvard charge, steadily grinding down Penn's lead. Over the last 200 meters, the lead seesawed back and forth on each stroke. With a thunderous sprint — and stroke Art Evans "going nuts" at the end — Harvard won, in a photo finish, by 0.05 seconds and went on to the Olympic Games in Mexico City.

A 2,000-meter eight-oared rowing race typically lasts between five and six minutes. When margins of victory are less than one second, probability suggests that a given crew should win about half these races and lose the other half. But that emphatically has not been the case when Harvard has been one of the crews. Quite the contrary: Harvard seems to win almost all its close races, the ones that reflect the fastest competition. Over the years, Harry Parker's varsities must have won twenty races by a total of 100 feet. Random chance cannot explain this.

The boat that wins close races is often the one that is coming from behind, not the one that is leading. Harvard does a lot of work on finishing very fast, which gets more emphasis than start-

ing. Over the years, there have been certain crews whose temperament favored grabbing the lead early, then seeking to maintain or
extend that lead for the rest of the race. But the classic Harvard
race plan has been: don't worry about getting ahead early, keep a
steady pace, then finish extremely hard. Most crews are not
coached that way. Facing Harvard, they are usually the underdogs;
they'd start extremely hard, get a lead, then get overexcited and
expend themselves in the middle 1,000 meters trying to stay ahead.

There is another factor involved. Each individual has a way of
rowing that will be most effective for that person. Generally, a crew
must row in unison, but the real trick may be to find people who
also row effectively in their own way. While certain technical elements — like having all the oarblades catch the water at once —
are universal, Parker may insist less on technical uniformity than
other coaches.

Recall Art Evans "going nuts" in the 1968 Olympic trial. There
are many coaches who, if the rowers start to "go nuts" — to do
things that are stylistically odd, trying to make the boat go fast —
will stop them from doing it. They emphasize a standard coaching
axiom: "Don't let your technique deteriorate." In contrast, with
Parker you can throw all caution to the winds as long as you are
making the boat go. Consider what in weight lifting they call *recruitment* — bringing into play other muscles that are nearby, or
are related to, the muscle you are working on a certain lift. In
weight lifting this is a sin because the target muscle is no longer
isolated. Yet, at the end of a race, you might try something like
recruitment: though it may be inefficient, you just want to get a
little more horsepower onto that oar. Harvard's oarsmen have
experimented more with those inefficient but effective short-term
strategies. When the whole crew does it, things aren't falling apart
— they are *all going nuts.* This collective insanity may squeeze out
enough extra boat speed to get Harvard's bow ball across the finish
line earlier — say, perhaps, 0.05 seconds earlier.

In the heat of the race, then, the Harvard oarsmen do not aim to capture any ideal of form or technique. Rather, they are in a state of abandon, most vehemently expressing themselves. It is the disciplined expression of *self* — not of technique — that wins races.

The row to the starting line is a long one. Launching from Cambridge Boat Club, I have a 2½-mile downstream journey ahead of me. In race-day traffic, crossing the river to reach the travel lane can be hazardous. Earlier today an elderly physician from the Midwest, who had borrowed one of our club singles for the Head, unwisely tried to cross the Charles amid oncoming race traffic and was hit by a four at full speed and taken to the hospital in an ambulance. Boat and doctor were both hurt but will recover. Foolish, self-destructive moves like darting out into river traffic indicate how race-day nerves can fry the circuits of judgment.

Today I will keep a cool head: I will not waste time fighting brushfires. I have readied myself in large ways over the past few months, but have also prepared for the smaller details that arise on race day: getting to the river and parking amid 250,000 spectators (take a bicycle); choosing what clothes to race in, when and where to change (club locker room); reserving my boat and oars for the race (well in advance, in the club logbook); food (a light breakfast, Harry Parker's race-day favorite: tea and toast); when to launch (my race starts at 12:24 P.M., so I plan to launch around 11:30 to be on the safe side).

Handling these details in advance means that they do not compete for my attention on regatta day. With fewer things to think about, it becomes easier to focus on the race. Like meditation, preparation empties the mind, improves the signal-to-noise ratio. We quiet the body by first extinguishing mental brushfires.

A regatta is like opening night at the theater, except there is only one performance. Hence as racers we may be able to learn something from how an actor prepares. Strong stage performances require that an actor learn the role "cold," in terms of spoken lines, cues, and stage blocking. Solid preparation frees energy for emotional expression.

I once wrote and performed a one-act play with two other actors. Just before our first performance, one of my fellow cast members anxiously asked me for any tips to help overcome self-consciousness onstage. I suggested that she try what I had been taught: focus on the other actors, relate and respond to *them*. Since she had prepared thoroughly, she was able to redirect her attention in this way. With the focus off herself, she brought spontaneity to the role. In much the same way, a well-prepared sculler can put attention where it matters on race day — not on self-evaluation but on the feel of the boat, the course, the water: relate and respond to *them*.

Today, every boathouse on the river swarms with activity, none more so than Cambridge Boat Club, host of the regatta. Celebratory burgees fly from our clubhouse roof. The verandah and grassy lawns are alive with members and guests. A constant flow of shells moves back and forth between the boat bays and the dock; from half a mile overhead, the clubhouse must resemble an anthill that transports racing shells instead of crumbs of food.

Yet the dock is small, with room for, at most, two singles on each side. To get one's shell off the rack, down the ramp, and into the water is the first challenge. The competition begins long before the race. This lesson was drummed into me repeatedly this fall as I vied with a score of scullers, all seeking to launch from the club dock at 5:45 A.M. We must assert ourselves amid this multitude; if we "wait for a good opening," we will find there *is* no good opening until everyone else has shoved off. We will be last off the dock, late to the start. Victory in the naval battle begins on dry land.

So at around 11:30 A.M. I hoist my shell overhead and bull my way down the ramp, put my boat into the water, push off from the dock, and begin paddling downstream. The warm-up ritual is a palladium, a sanctuary from pre-race terror: *Paddle four minutes, then four minutes of half pressure at 18, three minutes at 20, two at 22, one minute at 24.* Ritual prepares the body and distracts from the anxiety that inevitably arises at these moments when one's fate is about to be revealed.

In unpredictable environments, rituals provide a bit of turf that is under our control. We use the known to prepare for the unknown. Thus the baseball batter repeats a sequence of gestures before stepping into the box to hit. Close-order drill and the pervasive regimentation of military life create routines that build a stable frame of reference, a bulwark against the unpredictable. Such preparation may later mean survival when the chaos of battle is unleashed.

The October sun fans warmth through the air's crispness. A mile into my warm-up I find myself rowing alongside Lisa Stone, a friend and former Radcliffe coach. Lisa has just shoved off from the Weld dock on her way to the women's half of the Senior Masters Single race. I notice that she has bow #1: Lisa will be the first woman to start. Bow #1 typically signifies the previous year's winner, so I ask Lisa if she is planning to repeat as champion. She smiles and shakes her head demurely. "No, no, I don't expect to be fast today," she says. "I haven't trained too hard this year." *Well, I guess that makes two of us. Anyway, I probably haven't trained very hard by Lisa's standards. But I'm bow #39.* (Later, the race results expose Lisa's self-deprecating posture, when she repeats as champion — by a whopping twelve seconds.)

Just downstream from the Boston University Boathouse, the river widens dramatically. Sailboats often ply this area, called the

Charles River Basin. The basin makes an excellent marshaling area for the regatta, allowing the fifty men's shells and eleven more women's entrants in our event to continue their warm-ups while headed toward all compass points. There is enough room for chaos without collisions.

The chaos gradually arranges itself into order. Like iron filings under a magnetic field, all the shells start pointing upstream as 12:24 P.M. draws near. The starter calls the first boat to the line. Since the boats start ten seconds apart, with bow #39, it will still be more than six minutes before I cross the starting line in front of the Boston University Boathouse. Through the loudspeaker, I hear the starter calling the names of some of the most famous masters rowers alive. *"Bow #8, Mr. Spousta, please approach the start." "Bow #19, Mr. Dietz, ROW!"* Spousta holds the course record for this event. Jim Dietz was the U.S. national sculling champion through most of the 1970s. *These guys are in my race,* I think, and then: *What am I doing here?*

As the bow numbers get higher — *Bow #24, Mr. Melcher, please approach the start* — my heart rate inches up along with them. I maneuver my shell into the course alignment I want. Just 100 meters past the start, the Head course goes through the second arch of the Boston University Bridge, which includes a railroad trestle. (This is the only place in the world where a boat can scull beneath a train passing under a car driving below an airplane.) I get well out in the river and aim my bow at that second arch; my steering point is the northwest corner of the tallest building on the Boston skyline, the John Hancock skyscraper. I paddle lightly until I hear, *"Bow #39, Mr. Lambert, approach the start,"* and firm it up. As my shell nears the starting line I gather speed — keeping that Hancock tower on the stern — and then hear, *"Mr. Lambert, ROW!"* and so begin the Head of the Charles.

The task is to row my race. In this sense I am in a lane of my own, steering toward a destination I share with no one else. Yet I also have some objective goals. One is to stay ahead of whoever is rowing bow #40, at least until I am through the B.U. Bridge, to avoid the indignity of being passed within sight of the starting line. Fueled by the anaerobic god, I soon achieve this goal. *That's a win. O.K.* Beyond the bridge, however, some shells hurtle past me as we enter the wide swing by Magazine Beach and pass the friendly, sagging face of Riverside Boat Club. Rowing at a steady 26, I settle into a cadence I can sustain. I would not exactly call this swing, but I have found a groove, a rocking rhythm that allows me to breathe deeply and take long strokes. *Row big.*

The river straightens and I head toward the River Street Bridge, into the powerhouse stretch. I cruise along, keeping my shoulders low. *This is already starting to hurt.* Nearly a mile gone. Weariness inhabits my muscles, thanks to accumulating blood lactate, but the oxygen-burning system is working well: breathing very hard, yet not sucking wind.

I approach Weeks Bridge, a footbridge at what is, strategically, the most crucial turn on the course and the one most often muffed by out-of-towners. To swing it properly, you have to start turning early and angle the boat through the center arch, pointing toward the Boston shoreline on the other side and coming almost close enough to the bridge abutment to graze it with your oarblade. There isn't much traffic near me now, and I get my hull pointed exactly where I want it as I reel in the bridge.

From the riverbank, a familiar, booming voice resounds: "Way to go, Craig, you're steering a *great course!*" It is Tom Tiffany, and, well, he should know a great course when he sees one. Despite the size of the crowd, it is amazing how clearly we can single out friends' voices. Along the way, several of my other rooters add heartening yells, dosing me with their enthusiasm. If nothing else, these cheers momentarily distract me from the ongoing bodily pain, a most useful bonus. The crowd does matter.

I rock on, past Weld Boathouse, recalling mornings there with Community Rowing, ten years ago. Passing Newell, I remember coxing the Harvard freshmen in the fall of 1965. *This is where it began.* My rowing history is recapitulating itself as I make my way up the course. Out of the corner of my eye, in front of Newell, I glimpse Harry Parker, magisterial at the top of the ramp, and recall that Harry's middle name is Lambert. I take a power ten for Harry.

The two-mile mark recalls the 1985 Head, when Tiffany and I manned the two-mile umpiring station, spotting infractions with binoculars and relaying them to official headquarters via walkie-talkie. In the 1986 Head, when we reached this point in the double, I remember thinking, *Don't* tell *me there's another mile to go.*

Today I'm in better shape for that last mile. I inhale as much fall air as possible as I steer an aggressive course around the long turn that approaches Cambridge Boat Club. *Keep the strokes long and the course short.* Right beside the buoy line, I am rowing with my port oar over the buoys. This is perfectly legal: as long as my hull remains on the course, the oars can dig into any water they like. Then I hear it: *thump.* I instantly know I have run over a buoy. *Damn. Maybe nobody saw that.* Yet I know perfectly well that nearby, hawk-eyed umpires have binoculars trained on my shell and are already on their mobile phone, reporting my buoy infraction. No time to brood on it: I quickly pull hard on port, swinging the shell into the course to avoid missing the next buoy; each violation adds a ten-second penalty to my time.

As I approach Cambridge Boat Club, the cheers of friends and fellow club members warm my heart. Ed Jans is announcing this event, and his deep voice echoes through the public address system, audible for a hundred yards in both directions: "*Number 39 is Craig Lambert, from the home team, Cambridge Boat Club.*

[Cheers!] *Craig started reporting on rowing and liked it so much, he took it up himself a few years ago. He's rowing his first Head in the single, and by God, he looks pretty good out there."* Passing the club, I try to improve my form, just as I used to do years ago when I was smitten with a beautiful poet whose residence overlooked the river. I always hoped that someday she might notice me. Sometimes we can inspire ourselves by playing to an audience, even an imaginary one.

Then through the Eliot Bridge, the scene of the squeeze play a few weeks back when three scullers converged on me like torpedoes. Today I have the arch to myself. Half a mile to go. Very tired for the last mile. I am asking hurting muscles to keep going hard, and as predicted, they are objecting: *no more.* I focus only on the current stroke. "Pain does not matter to a man," wrote Hemingway. *Well, Ernie, actually, it does matter.* But we can row around pain or through it. Now I am sucking wind; my lungs thirst for air and greedily capture any oxygen molecules they can. *If only I had four lungs I could really make this shell fly.* Is that how the fish do it?

Headstones in a cemetery high on the Cambridge riverbank loom on port, signaling that the finish is near. *Four lungs or only two, let's go out hard.* I raise my rate to 32 for the final sprint. The shell surges under me; my lungs feel about to burst like an overinflated balloon. Lord knows how my form is now, but for this last stretch, this powerhouse stretch, I give up restraint, abandon myself to a perfect fusion of energy and pain, exhaustion and ecstasy. *Mind over water.*

Afterward, drenched in sweat, I paddle the half mile back to the boathouse. There I take my boat out of the water, dry its hull, stow my oars, and return the shell to its rack. I do not own this boat; it is one of our club's fleet, built of mahogany by Graeme King in Putney, Vermont, in 1981 and named the *Arthur Smithies,* after a former club member. I muse on the fact that Arthur is my middle name. Smithies had a legendary final row. The story goes that he was visited by a stroke or heart failure on the river, rowed to shore, and crawled up onto the riverbank, where he died. I wonder if this is the boat he went out in. In the race today, at times it felt like *I* was breathing my last. Yet I was going strong at the finish, and, perhaps, so was Arthur Smithies.

Later in the afternoon the results go up on the bulletin board. One sculler scratched from my event, so only forty-nine of us rowed the Senior Masters Single. My time over the course was 24:06.52, not a personal best, but one of the better times I've pulled in recent weeks. My buoy violation adds its penalty, so my adjusted official time is 24:16.52 — good for forty-sixth place and more than five minutes (or 27.3 percent) behind the winner, a Californian who finished in 19:04.48. Without my buoy penalty, I would have placed forty-fifth. I take some satisfaction in knowing that I beat four scullers up the course, even if forty-four others beat me. Seven other entrants in my event were also assessed penalties, mostly for buoys, including one particularly disastrous buoy infraction that moved a Canadian rower from first place to second and made the Californian this year's winner.

Later I calculate that about 89 percent of the scullers rowed the course faster than I did. Yes, I made the normal curve. *Yes, I can play with the big boys.* I am in the bottom 11 percent of the race, and yet, today, I am surely one of the winners.

On another Sunday in October, but in a different year and on a different river, I am about to row another three-mile head race. The Green Mountain Head in Putney, Vermont, is a small race limited to single and double sculls. Its entry form lists only two rules: "Bow balls required. No swearing." Near the space for age, it admonishes, "No cheating." This race is famous for its regional prizes: maple syrup for first place, bag of apples for second, cider for third. Despite the light touch, the Green Mountain attracts a strong field of scullers, a field that I chose to weaken slightly by joining it.

In Putney, the Connecticut River's high banks rise steeply like cathedral walls, enclosing us. No vaulted ceiling but a sky, misted over now by a morning haze that the sun warms from the other side. Already we feel the rays, even if we do not yet see the light. The protection of the high banks means glassy-flat water, ideal conditions. As I scull away from the tiny dock, the river feels like syrup against the oarblades.

I look upstream. Between the wooded banks, plumes of mist rise majestically from the river surface. It is a Wagnerian scene; I can almost hear the opening bars of *Tannhäuser.* Beautiful as it is, the mist also suggests the kind of temptation Odysseus might have encountered, since fog veils the upstream course, seducing us perhaps to row into chaos, collision, or onto rocks. Yet the morning fog is both curse and blessing: it confines us to the present moment because we cannot see ahead. So we must simply do an excellent job of being on course right now and trust that the future will take care of itself.

The pursuit of long-term goals can resemble climbing a mountain in a dense fog. Imagine climbing through a fog so thick that you cannot see beyond your next step. You have no idea how much farther there is to go. Under these conditions, the key is simply to make each step a sound one, and to keep going. Never cease moving upward, because your next step may be the one that places you on the summit.

During the race the sun finally burns off the mist, and we have a spectacular regatta on a superb New England fall day. I record a good time, but the day is successful for another reason: rowing through that mist taught me something. Whenever I go out to row and come back having learned something on the water, that has been a successful trip. The river gods have surely blessed me, because so far, all my trips have been successful.

Twilight, said don Juan, is a crack between two worlds. Up at the catch, I spread my wings, setting my shell to fly across the water as, on a nearby dock, a cormorant poses, drying its black feathers.

Between sunlight and shadow, sky and the water's depths, between thoughts and those molecules that speak thoughts to the body, lies the vertex of creation. Our visible world records what has been made so far. The future abides, unformed, in consciousness. We inhabit that which exists, ready to give birth to that which does not.

I skim the river's surface, a window on two worlds. *A sky facing upward.* Perhaps the sky above is another such window and myself another kind of fish, swimming ahead, peering up at the surface. Below my hull flows the water's current, and beneath the current is stillness. I lean into the drive. Catch, drive, release, recovery, as in: *spring, summer, autumn, winter.* To my port side a perch splashes. The wake ripples away astern as my mind relaxes into the charm of that deep stillness, and solitude settles in. It is warm and quiet on this autumn evening, yet no one else is out. Tonight, the river is mine.

The finish of the rowing stroke, the release of blades from water, completes and begins a cycle: with the death of one impulse arises another. Release becomes recovery. I feather my blades and, on the inhale, glide softly up to the catch. The flowing sequence is an emblem of beauty and order. The stroke cycle and the life cycle are one.

There is no need for us to put the world in order. The world is in order; we need only align ourselves, to tune our souls to the order that already sustains us. Stillness gives rise to motion. Vibrations emerge from the silence, and so is the world formed. My oars connect me with these waves from the depths. Presence and rhythm are always there, awaiting the moment when we find each other. They are able to steer flawlessly, if only I trust them the rudder.

On the water, tinted by this October sunset, yes, presence and rhythm row my shell through the arch, into the powerhouse stretch. In the boat, stretched out at the catch, I balance on the cusp of two worlds. My wings on port and starboard beat together, and, on the exhale, we fly upstream, into the twilight.

ACKNOWLEDGMENTS

Three professional colleagues contributed uniquely to the creation of this book. As an editor, Marc Jaffe has been impeccable; his sound instincts and generosity of spirit were a sustaining influence at every stage of this project's evolution. Mindy Keskinen of Houghton Mifflin has been a delight to work with, bringing not only high professionalism but wit and enthusiasm to every interaction. I'm grateful for the integrity, accessibility, and savvy of my literary agent, Gordon Kato; his worldliness and sense of humor transform professional transactions into lively conversations.

Every creative work grows from the fabric of the author's life. In my case that fabric has been woven by many cherished friends who, directly or indirectly, have enabled me to write my book. I am grateful to Ivonne A-Baki, Brad Addison, Marcia Banciu, Nancy Bennett, John T. Bethell, Eric Blumenson, Angel Cacciola, Bobbi Coogan, Charlie Davidson, Peter Desmond, Logynn Ferrall, Larry Fieman, Dave Fish, Gretchen Friesinger, Leslie Gabriele, Robert E. Ginna, Jr., Gerry Goodman, Jim Harrison, Richard F. Herbst, Lucinda Jewell, Greg Johnson, Stephanie Jones, Nancy Kelly, Katharine Kinderman, J. C. Louis, the Magnificent Seven, Denny and Tippy Makepeace, Karen Melikian, Cristina Dragomirescu Merrill, Cyndi Mitchell, Anan Nathif, John Newmeyer, Eva Nilsen, Bill Novak, Stephen Prophet,

Acknowledgments

Thomas Putnam, Kit and Jane Reed, Katrina Roberts, Andrea Szmyt, Megan Makepeace Tarini, and David Updike.

Over the past three decades, I've been privileged to know many rowers and coaches who have generously shared their knowledge and passion for the sport with me. Those friends and acquaintances prove the truth of Frank Shields's maxim, "There's no such thing as a bad seat at a rowing dinner." My teachers include Clint Allen, Andy Anderson, Dan Bakinowski, Seth Bauer, Bill Becklean, the late Edward H. Bennett, Jr., Fred Borchelt, Joe Bouscaren, Dan Boyne, Steve Brooks, Dick Cashin, Geoffrey Curtis, Tom Darling, Christopher Dodd, Bari, Peter, and Dick Dreissigacker, Malcolm Gefter, Carie Graves, Gordon Hamilton, Henry Hamilton, Charlie Hamlin, the late Thomi Keller, Sandy Kendall, Graeme King, Larry Klecatsky, Geoffrey Knauth, Brad Lewis, Ken Lynch, Sara Hall McCann, Will Melcher, Thomas Mendenhall, Holly Metcalf, Ted Nash, Thor Nilssen, Harry Parker, Dickie Perelli, Hart Perry, Whitney Post, Peter Raymond, Hartley Rogers, Allen P. Rosenberg, Frank Shields, Matt Smith, Kurt Somerville, Gregg Stone, Emily Talcott, Lawrence "Monk" Terry, Jr., Ted Van Dusen, Ted Washburn, and Tiff Wood.

The orbits of friendship and rowing conjoin in many places, but nowhere more significantly than in the person of Thomas D. Tiffany, cocaptain of the 1971 Harvard varsity crew and founding member of the Sesame Noodle Rowing Club and the International Federation of Sagittarian Coxwains. His attendance record is perfect for all meetings of both these organizations. Over the years, Tom has been my most consistent rowing mentor as well as a kindred spirit and incomparable friend.

In a life blessed with many sources of happiness, my family is the greatest gift I have received. Carol and Vincent Cortese, Jeffrey, Jillian, and Brooke Lambert, Nanette, Daniel, Adam, and Corinne Zucker, and my parents, L. William Lambert and Ruth K. Lambert, have given me infinite caring and support, while providing fine examples of how to live fully and with love. If this book reflects who I am, they are my coauthors.

Made in the USA
Lexington, KY
28 November 2018